Beyond the First Draft

Beyond the First Draft

Editing Strategies for Powerful Legal Writing

Megan McAlpin

CAROLINA ACADEMIC PRESS
Durham, North Carolina

Library of Congress Cataloging-in-Publication Data

McAlpin, Megan.
  Beyond the first draft : editing strategies for powerful legal writing /
Megan McAlpin.
      pages cm
  Includes bibliographical references and index.
  ISBN 978-1-59460-998-5 (alk. paper)
  1. Legal composition. I. Title.

  K94.M35 2013
  808.06'634--dc23   2013036663

CAROLINA ACADEMIC PRESS
700 Kent Street
Durham, NC 27701
Telephone (919) 489-7486
Fax (919) 493-5668
www.cap-press.com

Printed in the United States of America
2021 Printing

To Jay, the only person who is always certain that I can do what I think I cannot.

And to Jillian and Charlotte, for all of their patience and willingness to "help me with my letters."

Contents

Acknowledgments

I am so thankful to my colleagues, my students, and my family for everything that they contributed to this book.

First, I am grateful to my colleague Suzanne Rowe who took a chance on me so many years ago and who took her pink pen to every page of this book. There is no way I will ever be able to repay her.

I am also thankful to my colleagues Liz Frost, Joan Rocklin, and Anne Mullins who read portions of the book, provided feedback, and were willing to test my ideas with their students.

I also owe a debt of gratitude to several institutions. First, I am grateful to the Deans at my own institution, the University of Oregon School of Law, for providing me with research grants that allowed me to carve out the time to dedicate to this project. I am also grateful to the Association of Legal Writing Directors, which funded the Scholars' Workshop at which I was able to share some of my work with Kim Holst, Steve Johansen, and Valerie Munson. And of course, I am grateful to those three colleagues for their ideas and insights.

I am thankful, too, to the students who patiently worked their way through the first drafts of this book and provided feedback. I owe special thanks to research assistants Elayna Zammarelli, Lindsay Massara, and Clint Burke who looked carefully at each chapter and shared their thoughts and ideas.

Perhaps most importantly, I am grateful to my family for the sacrifices they made to make this book possible. My parents, Forrest and Karen Bell, spent many years investing in me as a student and a writer. My husband, Jay McAlpin, spent many long evenings and weekends caring for our two young daughters to make it possible for me to write. He also spent many long hours convincing me that I could, in fact, finish this book. And I am grateful to my girls, Jillian and Charlotte, who were patient with me and who I hope will someday read this book and know how valuable that patience was.

Beyond the First Draft

Chapter 1

Writing and Rewriting

"I'm not a very good writer, but I'm an excellent rewriter."
—James Michener

"Half my life is an act of revision." — *John Irving*

Very good legal writing is a product of rewriting. In fact, most good writing is a product of rewriting. In her book *Bird by Bird*, Anne Lamott wrote: "Almost all good writing begins with terrible first efforts. You need to start somewhere."

In legal writing, even before you can begin to write your "terrible first effort," you have to understand your client's problem, the law that governs it, and the hoped for outcome. You have to research, analyze, and organize the cases and statutes that you find and decide how those cases and statutes affect your client. Once you have done all this, you are ready to write your first draft.

Getting to the first draft is difficult analytical work.[1] But getting to the first draft is really just the beginning of the hard work. First drafts are not enough; you are a lawyer, and someone is paying you to write. You are writing to someone else, be that another attorney, a client, or a judge. And you are writing on behalf of a client for whom the stakes are high. So even if your "terrible first effort" is actually pretty good, a first effort is simply not enough. You must go beyond the first draft.

Going beyond the first draft is more than just proofreading what you have written. There is a fundamental difference between proofreading and rewriting. Proofreading is the final thing you do to perfect your work. But rewriting is what happens between the first draft and the final

> **Learning to Think Like a Writer**
>
> Law professors will often tell you that you learn to "think like a lawyer" in law school. And you do. You also learn an entirely new vocabulary (think: negligence, consideration, *mens rea*).
>
> But lawyers, as much as anything else, are writers. As important as it is to understand the language of lawyers, it is just as important to understand the language of writers (think: phrase, dependent clause, comma).
>
> Sometimes, the language of writers is grammar. So, in this book, you will see that the first time a grammatical term is used, it is defined in a sidebar. For easy reference, all of those grammar reminders are also collected in an appendix at the back of the book.

---

1. This book assumes that you have an analytically sound, logically organized first draft. If you are not there yet, you need to take that first step.

draft that just needs to be proofed. The goal in rewriting is to turn your first draft, which is clear and organized to you as the writer, into a second (or third or fourth or fifth) draft that is clear and organized to your reader.

The best rewriting is done in steps. In fact, the best rewriting is a little like cleaning. When you clean a room, you start by picking up all the pizza boxes (or, depending on your house, the shoes or clothes or toys) on the floor. Once you have done that, you vacuum the rug. If you started with the vacuum, not only would the rug not actually get clean but the pizza boxes wouldn't get picked up either. Because rewriting, like cleaning, works best taken step by step, this book is organized around the steps of the rewriting process. The next chapter focuses on coherence, the third on vigor, the fourth on clarity, and the final on polish. Each step is separate and distinct. If you try to polish before your writing is coherent, you're just taking a vacuum to a floor full of pizza boxes.

This book takes the steps of rewriting one at a time, but it is not necessarily meant to be read cover to cover; it is meant to be used as a reference. You will see that each chapter begins with a checklist to use as you take on that stage of the rewriting process. Start with the checklist. If you need more detail on any of the items in the checklist, turn to the corresponding section in the chapter to find a more detailed explanation along with samples and strategies for improving your draft.

A word of warning about the more detailed sections of the chapters: they are, well, detailed. In fact, these sections will require you to tackle some grammatical terms that you may have avoided until this point in your life. But anyone who can understand and master the legal rule against perpetuities can certainly understand and master the grammatical rules of relative pronouns. Actually, knowing the ins and outs of the rule against perpetuities won't do you much good if you can't then write about that rule in a coherent, vigorous, clear, and polished way.

The good news, of course, is that your first draft doesn't have to be coherent, vigorous, clear, or polished. The first draft is for you — the goal is simply to get the law onto the page. So, go ahead, write that first draft. And don't worry if it's a terrible first effort. It's *supposed* to be a terrible first effort. Just make sure that you don't stop at that first draft. Instead, use the strategies in this book to begin the process of rewriting. At every stage of that rewriting process, your "terrible first effort" will improve until it becomes very good legal writing.

Chapter 2

Coherent Writing

"Easy reading is damn hard writing." — Nathaniel Hawthorne

One of the most difficult things about legal writing is that you — the writer — must take a jumble of very complex information and organize it in a logical way. Then, to achieve coherent writing, you have to make the organization obvious to your reader.

Your first draft creates organization. It is the draft that allows you to make sense of that jumble of information. You marshal together all of the relevant legal authorities, explain them, and analyze them. Your first draft may help you discover things about the law or about your facts that you weren't able to see before you began writing. In that way, the first draft is very powerful for you. It is the working draft.

But the first draft is just for you. While you have made order out of the chaos in the first draft, you still need to make the order that you've created obvious to your reader. And that's what the second (or, more likely, thirteenth) draft is for. You must go beyond the first draft to turn a draft that feels organized to you into a final product that your reader will *perceive* as organized. This second (or thirteenth) draft is the coherence draft.

The difference between organized writing and coherent writing is one of reader perception. Organized writing is writing that has a logical order (think: separated out into elements or factors, issues or arguments). Coherent writing is not only logically organized, but it also makes that organization apparent to the reader. Coherent writing is writing that your reader *experiences* as organized because he is able to move from one idea to the next without stumbling or becoming disoriented.

To turn organized writing into coherent writing, you must (1) provide clear introductions to new information and (2) provide transitions to help your reader move from sentence to sentence, idea to idea, and paragraph to paragraph without "discernible bumps, gaps, or shifts."[1]

Turning organized writing into coherent writing is, without a doubt, a rewriting task. Again, the strategies in this chapter are not about how to organize your analysis. They are about how to make your organization clear to your reader. The process of organizing your analysis — into separate elements or factors — is the first, analytical step. Only once you have created a logical organization in your first draft can you begin to make that organization clear to your reader. After all, introductory paragraphs, topic sentences, and transitions do not create organization. They are simply tools for helping your reader understand the organization that is already there.

---

1. Diana Hacker, *The Bedford Handbook* 91 (7th ed. 2009).

Coherent Writing:
The Editing Checklist

1. Provide Introductions

✍ 2.1 Check the Beginning of Each Section of Your Document for an Introduction

Look at the beginning of each section of your document and make sure that you have introduced your reader to both the topic and structure of that section.

✍ 2.2 Check the Beginning of Each New Legal Analysis or Argument for an Introduction

Look at the beginning of each discrete part of your legal analysis and make sure that you have introduced your reader to the topic and structure of that analysis.

✍ 2.3 Check the Beginning of Each Paragraph for a Topic Sentence

Look at the beginning of each new paragraph and make sure that you have introduced your reader, at a minimum, to the topic of the paragraph.

2. Provide Transitions

✍ 2.4 Check for Transitional Words and Phrases

Carefully read each paragraph and make sure that you have included appropriate transitional words and phrases — both between paragraphs and between sentences within the paragraph — to demonstrate the relationship between ideas.

✍ 2.5 Check for Substantive Transitions

Carefully read each paragraph and decide whether a substantive transition might be more helpful or appropriate for demonstrating the relationship between two ideas.

3. Creating Organization Before Coherence

Coherent Writing:
The Details

1. Provide Introductions

An old adage provides advice to public speakers: tell your audience what you're going to tell them; tell them; then tell them what you told them. It's actually pretty good advice for legal writers as well. One of the most important things you can do to turn organized writing into coherent writing is to tell your audience what you're going to tell them, by using introductions. (There are also times when a good, concise conclusion — telling your readers what you told them — might also be a good idea.)

This simple advice works because, as readers, we understand information best if we are able to grasp its significance as soon as we read it.[2] To understand how important it is for a reader to be able to grasp information as she reads, consider, for a minute, the mystery novel. Mystery writers very purposefully leave their readers in the dark. They don't want their readers to be able to grasp the significance of every piece of information as they read. Think of the last mystery novel you read. On page 362, when you discovered that the butler did it, you were floored. And then you started to make sense of all the little clues that you'd missed along the way. The red shoe that was important. The letter that the butler hid from Ms. Scarlett was really an indicator of his guilt, too. And now (oh, the excitement!), you simply must go back and read the whole book from the beginning.

The whole point, of course, is that the reader of a mystery novel doesn't *want* to be told what she's going to be told. She doesn't want to easily grasp the significance of each fact as she reads. She wants to have to work hard to figure out the mystery and to be surprised at the end. The legal reader, on the other hand, *needs* to easily grasp the significance of each fact as she reads. She doesn't want to work hard to discern the writer's meaning, and she doesn't want to be surprised at the end. She doesn't want to have to go back and read the whole memo or motion from the beginning. And it's the writer's job to make sure she doesn't have to.

Think again about that mystery novel with the badly behaved butler. To turn it into the fact statement of a memo, you would begin by telling your reader that the butler is probably guilty and that two facts point to this guilt: (1) the red shoe and (2) the letter the butler hid from Ms. Scarlett. By providing your reader with this introduction to the facts she's about to read before launching into the details of those facts, you've

---

2. Stephen V. Armstrong & Timothy P. Terrell, *Thinking Like a Writer: A Lawyer's Guide to Effective Writing and Editing* 18 (3d ed. 2009).

made it possible for her to focus on the important details when she gets there.

So, to turn organized writing into coherent writing, you need to be sure that, at every step along the way, you tell your reader what you're going to tell her. In other words, you need to make sure that you are including an introduction whenever one is necessary.

Knowing when an introduction is necessary is a bit more art than science. But one rule of thumb can help you decide whether an introduction is necessary: you need to include an introduction any time you are giving your reader new information, especially if that information is at all complicated. While you are the only one who will know for sure whether you are introducing new information, there are a few places in any document where you are inevitably going to be introducing new information: (1) the beginning of each new section of a document (e.g., the statement of facts, the discussion section), (2) the beginning of each new piece of legal analysis or argument, and (3) the beginning of (almost) every new paragraph.

✎ Editing Strategy 2.1
Check the Beginning of Each Section of Your Document for an Introduction

---

Each time a writer begins a new section of a document, he is inevitably introducing his reader to new information. So, as you edit, check the beginning of each new section of your document (e.g., the statement of facts, the discussion section) to be sure that you've effectively introduced your reader to what is about to come.

An effective introduction will look a little different depending on the type of document that you are writing (memo, letter, brief) and the section within that document that you are editing (statement of facts, discussion section). However, almost all effective introductions do two things: (1) introduce the reader to the topic of the document or section and (2) introduce the reader to the structure of the document or section.

To introduce your reader to your topic, you simply need to tell her what she's going to read about—negligence, assault—and why it's important—your client has a claim for negligence, your client may be liable for assault. To introduce your reader to your structure, you need to tell your reader about the organization she's about to encounter—a discussion of negligence split into five parts—and where to pay close attention—the second part, where things get complicated.

To get a sense of the importance of an introduction, consider the following scenario. Your supervisor has asked you to determine whether your client, Ms. Stark, can establish a prima facie case of retaliatory discharge under Michigan's whistle-blower's protection act. You've done all the research and discovered statutes and cases on point. You've read those statutes and cases, pulled them apart, analyzed them, and discovered that your client will have to establish three elements in order to prevail. You've then gone beyond this analysis to really look at your client's facts and have decided that she probably can prevail but that she will struggle with one of the elements. You've written all of this in your first draft. (Actually, if you're being honest with yourself, it took you six drafts, not one.) And, even though you really struggled with the law at first, you've now become an expert. It's all very clear to you, and you have a draft that is organized logically.

Your memo begins with the obligatory discussion heading, and then you dive right in to the discussion section. Your memo starts like Example 2.1(a).

Example 2.1(a)
Discussion section of a memo with an ineffective introductory paragraph

Draft: The first issue is whether Ms. Stark can show that she was engaged in a protected activity. An employee can establish that she is engaged in a protected activity if she can show that ...

Your memo is shaping up to be a very good mystery novel. Your use of the words *first issue* gives your reader a clue that there is more than one issue. But to find out how many issues, she'll have to read to the end. Your reader also knows that Ms. Stark will have to show that she engaged in a protected activity, but you're building suspense by refusing to tell your reader whether Ms. Stark can in fact demonstrate this element.

While you have the makings of a mystery novel, you're not writing a mystery novel, so you need to provide your reader with an introduction. Example 2.1(b) shows how an introductory paragraph can be an effective tool for telling your reader what you're going to tell her.

Example 2.1(b)
Discussion section of a memo with an effective introductory paragraph

Revised: Ms. Stark can establish a prima facie case of retaliatory discharge under Michigan's whistle-blower's protection act. To establish a prima facie case of retaliatory discharge, an employee must show that (1) she was engaged in a protected activity, (2) she was discharged,

> and (3) a causal connection existed between the
> protected activity and the discharge. *Henry v. City of*
> *Det.*, 594 N.W.2d 107, 110 (Mich. App. 1999). Ms.
> Stark can easily demonstrate that she was engaged in a
> protected activity and that she was discharged, but she
> will have some difficulty in demonstrating the causal
> connection between the protected activity and the
> discharge. Ultimately, however, Ms. Stark should
> prevail.

This introduction provides your reader with everything that she needs in order to fully engage with the analysis that is ahead of her. It's like a roadmap of the car trip she's about to take. First, you've introduced her to the topic. She knows what she's about to read: an analysis of retaliatory discharge. She also knows why it's important: the client can establish a prima facie case. Second, you've introduced her to the structure. She can anticipate the organization she's about to encounter: a three-part elemental analysis. Finally, she knows where she should pay close attention: to the analysis of a causal connection between the protected activity and the discharge.

GPS and Specific Accurate Maps

The roadmap analogy might be a little out of date. After all, it's more likely that you actually rely on a Google map for specific directions or the GPS in your car to give you turn-by-turn directions to get you to your destination. If you do in fact use a GPS, it's probably because that GPS is likely to be both more specific (you can make it take you exactly where you want to go) and, at least arguably, more accurate. There's really nothing more frustrating than an out-of-date map that can't help you get exactly where you're going.

The same is true in your writing. Your reader is going to get frustrated really quickly if the introduction you give her doesn't accurately map the content that follows. In other words, if your introduction suggests that you will be talking first about protected activity, then about discharge, and finally about the causal connection between the protected activity and the discharge, you had better do just that. Don't talk about discharge, then protected activity, then causation. Changing the order on your reader will make your reader feel like she's using an out-of-date, useless map. She won't trust it and she'll be frustrated. Make sure that you give her the GPS turn-by-turn directions instead.

Of course, introductions aren't always structured exactly like the introduction in Example 2.1(b). Examples 2.1(c) and 2.1(d) demonstrate appropriate introductions for the beginning of a letter to Ms. Stark and the beginning of an e-mail to your supervisor.

Example 2.1(c)
Effective introductory paragraph in a client letter

Revised: It was a pleasure to meet with you the other day. I have now researched whether you have a claim against your former employer for firing you after you took steps to report the employer's use of lead paint in schools. I believe that you have a good argument that your employer discharged you as retaliation for your actions, which is prohibited by Michigan law. Below, I describe the facts as I understand them and my analysis.

Example 2.1(d)
Effective introductory paragraph in an e-mail to a supervisor

Revised: Last week, you asked whether Julie Stark can establish a prima facie case of retaliatory discharge under Michigan's whistle-blower's protection act. The answer is yes, she can.

While these introductions may seem, at first glance, to be very different, they have two things in common. They each (1) introduce the reader to the topic of the document and (2) introduce the reader to the structure of the document.

While the introductions do have some differences, those differences really only reflect the different purposes and audiences of the documents. For instance, the introductions that are written for other lawyers include a detailed description of the governing rule, while the introduction that is written for a client doesn't. In addition, the introduction in the memo is much more detailed than the introduction in the e-mail because the analysis in the memo is likely much more developed than the analysis in the e-mail. Ultimately, all of the introductions provide essentially the same information, just tailored to the specific audience and type of document.

The Last Thing You Write:
The Secret to Writing Great Introductions

Here's a helpful tip for writing a great introduction: write it last. The best introductions, whether they're introductory paragraphs or topic sentences, tell your reader what you're going to tell them. So it makes sense that you have to know what you're going to tell your reader before you can write a great introduction. In your early drafts, don't worry about writing your introduction. Once you know what you're going to tell your reader, go back and write the introduction.

If you're still struggling to write a good introduction, look at the end of whatever you've written. For example, if you're struggling to write a good topic sentence, look at the very last sentence in the paragraph. There's a pretty good chance that you've ended the paragraph with a summary. Tweak it a little bit and move it to the front of the paragraph and you'll have a great topic sentence. For an example of how this works, take a look at the revision sentences in Examples 2.3(a) and (b). Do you notice how the topic and concluding sentences are similar?

Just as an introduction will vary based on the type of document and the audience, introductions also vary based on the particular section of the document. Example 2.1(b) demonstrated how the discussion section of a memo would begin. But there are other sections to memos, and briefs, and letters, and all sorts of documents that lawyers write every day.

While looking at samples of different kinds of introductions can be useful, there certainly is no template for writing an introduction. Instead, in every instance, the writer must make sure that he's telling his reader what she's going to read, why it's important, and what she'll encounter.

Example 2.1(e) demonstrates how the statement of facts of the retaliatory discharge memo might begin.

Example 2.1(e)
Effective introductory paragraph in a memo's statement of facts

Revised: Our client, Julie Stark, was discharged from her job as a project manager with the company Arnett & Plausen after she took steps to report the company for using lead-based paint in a school. Ms. Stark believes that she was discharged because she was about to report that the company was violating the law and has asked whether she has any legal recourse against the company.

In some ways, this introduction is less explicit than the introduction to the discussion section, but it still tells the reader what she's going to read (the story of Julie Stark who was fired by Arnett & Plausen, possibly as retaliation) and why it's important (we are representing Ms. Stark). While the introduction doesn't explicitly introduce the structure of the section, that works for a statement of facts, which a reader will expect to be chronologically organized.

CREAC

✍ Editing Strategy 2.2
Check the Beginning of Each New Legal Analysis
or Argument for an Introduction

While writing an introduction at the beginning of each section of a document is a good first step, it's not enough. You also need to include an introduction at the beginning of each discrete part of your legal analysis or argument (for example, each new element).

If you take a closer look at your first draft of that retaliatory discharge memo, you'll discover that you've written an analysis for each of the individual elements. Your discussion of the third element might begin like Example 2.2(a).

Example 2.2(a)
Individual element with an ineffective introduction

Draft: The final issue that a court will examine is whether a causal connection existed between the protected activity and the discharge. In one case, the Michigan Court of Appeals held that there was a causal connection between the employee's protected activity and the discharge. *Roulston v. Tendercare (Mich.), Inc.*, 608 N.W.2d 525, 530-31 (Mich. App. 2000).

Once again, you've done what the writer of any early draft would do: you've begun by defining the issue and then diving into the cases that will help you understand the issue. But surely your thinking has progressed beyond this early draft, and you need to allow your reader to take full advantage of that thinking. So, you once again need to provide your reader with an introduction—this time for the individual issue. You'll do that by providing the kind of introduction that appears in Example 2.2(b).

Example 2.2(b)
Individual element with an effective introduction

Revision: Finally, Ms. Stark will be able to demonstrate the causal connection between her protected activity and her discharge. To prove a causal connection between protected activity and discharge, an employee must show (1) that the employer had objective notice that the plaintiff had engaged in a protected activity and (2) additional evidence, beyond objective notice, that links the notice to the discharge. *See West v. GMC*, 665

> N.W.2d 468, 472 (Mich. App. 2003). However, even if the employee is able to prove both of these elements, the employer can still argue that the plaintiff acted in bad faith. *Shallal v. Catholic Soc. Servs. of Wayne Co.*, 566 N.W.2d 571, 579 (Mich. 1997). If the court determines the plaintiff acted in bad faith, the court will hold that no causal connection exists. *Id.*

This introduction begins with a conclusion about the particular element and then moves to the governing rule for that element. It may look simply like a typical Conclusion and Rule that would begin any CREAC (or IRAC or IREAC or CREXAC or whatever it is you call it—you get the point). That's because it is. Actually, one of the reasons that the CREAC paradigm works so well is that it forces a writer to begin with the kind of introductory material that the reader needs before diving into the analysis.

By providing that introductory material to the single element, you've allowed your reader to once again understand what she's about to read so that she can engage with the material immediately. Unlike Example 2.2(a), which hints at what your reader is going to read about but doesn't tell her why it's important, Example 2.2(b) gives her both pieces of information. And unlike Example 2.2(a), which doesn't give the reader any clue about the organization to come, Example 2.2(b) uses a governing rule to map out the structure of this part of the memo. The result is that, by providing the introduction to the element, you have made sure that writing that was already organized will now be *perceived* as organized by the reader. And that's really good writing.

✍ Editing Strategy 2.3
Check the Beginning of Each Paragraph for a Topic Sentence

Just as you will inevitably be introducing your reader to new information at the beginning of a new section of a document or the beginning of a new section of legal analysis, you will also inevitably be introducing your reader to new information at the beginning of a paragraph. After all, that's what paragraphs are for, right? Because you know that you'll be introducing your reader to new information at the beginning of each paragraph, you need to be sure that you've told your reader what to be ready for in that paragraph. So, when you are editing for coherence, check the beginning of each paragraph for a topic sentence.

A topic sentence, like an introductory paragraph, is simply an effective introduction. It introduces the reader to the topic of the paragraph by telling her what she's going to read about and why it's important. Sometimes, really good topic sentences even tell the reader about the organization she's about to encounter.

> ### Harnessing the Power of the Topic Sentence: The Topic Sentence Outline
>
> When you write, you always need to remember that you're writing not for you but for your reader. So it's always helpful to know a little something about that reader. Here are two things you should know about your reader: (1) she's busy and (2) she's *using* your writing — perhaps going back to it again and again as a resource — rather than just reading your writing.
>
> Because your reader is busy and trying to mine your writing for useful information, she sometimes starts by reading only your topic sentences. What does this mean for you? It means that your topic sentences need to be excellent. It also means that your reader should be able to understand your argument or explanation by reading *only* your topic sentences.
>
> To be sure that this will work, create a topic sentence outline. Take what you've written and highlight just the first sentence of each paragraph. Now, read just those sentences. Can you follow the argument or analysis? Is there something fundamentally missing? Does one of your paragraphs start with information that isn't really helpful?
>
> Creating a topic sentence outline will not only allow you to make sure that your reader will follow you easily, but it will also help you spot holes in your own analysis or argument. In fact, creating a topic sentence outline is a valuable exercise both in the editing stage and probably in the planning stage as well.

The next two examples show effective topic sentences in different parts of an objective memo. Example 2.3(a) comes from an objective memo on trade secret law. In the draft, the writer launches right into an illustration of a case — he lays out the facts, then the court's reasoning, and then the court's holding. This is a perfectly organized way to approach the case illustration. But the reader won't experience the case illustration as organized because she's walking into it blindly — she has no idea what she's about to read or why it's important. In the revision, the author puts that introductory information right up front in a topic sentence. In the revision, the writer is using the very first sentence to tell his reader what the paragraph will be about and why it's important.

Example 2.3(a)
Weak explanation paragraph revised by adding an effective topic sentence

Draft: In *Machen, Inc. v. Aircraft Design, Inc.*, 828 P.2d 73, 324 (Wash. App. 1992), the plaintiff corporation, Machen, claimed that several pieces of information made up a protectable trade secret. *Machen, Inc. v. Aircraft Design, Inc.*, 828 P.2d 73, 324 (Wash. App. 1992). This information included (1) knowledge that Piper Aerostar brakes were deficient, and (2) knowledge that a modified Beechcraft Duke brake would be a sufficient alternative. *Id.* One of Machen's former employees used this information to create a replacement brake for the Piper Aerostar for one of Machen's competitors. *Id.* at 322. The court held that the knowledge that the Piper Aerostar brake was deficient was generally known because, not only did the employee know the information even before he came to work for Machen, but Piper Aerostar's pilots, mechanics, and parts manufacturers knew the information as well. *Id.* at 325-26.

Revision: **Information is generally known when others in the industry are aware of it.** *Machen, Inc. v. Aircraft Design, Inc.*, 828 P.2d 73, 325 (Wash. App. 1992). In *Machen*, the plaintiff corporation, Machen, claimed that several pieces of information made up a protectable trade secret. *Id.* at 324. This information included (1) knowledge that Piper Aerostar brakes were deficient, and (2) knowledge that a modified Beechcraft Duke brake would be a sufficient alternative. *Id.* One of Machen's former employees used this information to create a replacement brake for the Piper Aerostar for one of Machen's competitors. *Id.* at 322. The court held that the knowledge that the Piper Aerostar brake was deficient was generally known because, not only did the employee know the information even before he came to work for Machen, but Piper Aerostar's pilots, mechanics, and parts manufacturers knew the information as well. *Id.* at 325-26.

Paragraph Blocks

When a topic is too big to be adequately covered in a single paragraph, you can use a paragraph block.

A paragraph block is a group of paragraphs that function together—the first paragraph in the block serves as the topic paragraph, the next paragraphs support that topic paragraph and, sometimes, a final paragraph serves as a conclusion.

In a paragraph block, not every paragraph will necessarily have its own topic sentence. Instead, the paragraphs will be unified by the initial paragraph in the block.

Example 2.3(b) comes from that same objective memo on trade secrets. Again, the draft paragraph is very logically organized. But the organization only becomes clear to the reader after she reads the topic sentence in the revision. That topic sentence tells the reader what she's about to read and why it's important. But the topic sentence in the revision is even more impressive because it also tells the reader about the organization she's about to encounter — first she'll read about the parts of the process and then about the process as a whole.

Example 2.3(b)
Weak paragraph in an application section revised by adding a topic sentence

Draft: Like the information in *Machen*, the partial short fermentation process is made up of several discrete pieces of information. One of these pieces is the knowledge that a shorter fermentation period makes sweeter wine. Like the employee in *Machen*, Ms. Hamilton knew this information before working for Mr. Russell. In addition, others in the winemaking industry are aware of this information, similar to the Piper Aerostar mechanics, pilots, and manufacturers in *Machen* who were aware of the brake deficiency. Therefore, the court will likely determine that the knowledge that a shorter fermentation period makes sweeter wine is generally known. However, like the drawings in *Boeing,* while the partial short fermentation process may include some information that is available elsewhere, the process as a whole is not generally known. Others in the wine industry have tried to discover Mr. Russell's process and have been unable to do so. This shows that others are not aware of all of the elements of the partial short fermentation process. Therefore, a court would likely determine that the partial short fermentation process is not generally known.

Revision: **The partial short fermentation process is not generally known because, while some in the winemaking industry are aware of parts of the process, no one in the industry has knowledge of the process as a whole.** Like the information in *Machen*, the partial short fermentation process is made up of several discrete pieces of information. One of these pieces is the knowledge that a shorter fermentation period makes sweeter wine. Like the employee in *Machen*, Ms. Hamilton knew this information before working for Mr. Russell. In addition, others in the winemaking industry are aware of this information, similar to the Piper

> Aerostar mechanics, pilots, and manufacturers in
> *Machen* who were aware of the brake deficiency.
> Therefore, the court will likely determine that the
> knowledge that a shorter fermentation period makes
> sweeter wine is generally known. However, like the
> drawings in *Boeing*, while the partial short fermentation
> process may include some information that is available
> elsewhere, the process as a whole is not generally
> known. Others in the wine industry have tried to
> discover Mr. Russell's process and have been unable to
> do so. This shows that others are not aware of all of the
> elements of the partial short fermentation process.
> Therefore, a court would likely determine that the
> partial short fermentation process is not generally
> known.

Of course, effective topic sentences come in all shapes and sizes, and some will look nothing like the examples above. Sometimes, a topic sentence is not express. Example 2.3(c) once again comes from that same trade secret memo. This time, though, the paragraph is from the memo's statement of facts. In the statement of facts, the writer relies on chronological order as his guiding organizational principle. He trusts that his reader will follow this chronological organization easily enough without express topic sentences. (In fact, in Example 2.3(c), the implied topic sentence will make the reader expect that the rest of the paragraph will be in chronological order.)

> **Example 2.3(c)**
> **Implied topic sentence in a statement of facts**
>
> Revision: Before joining Snohomish Winery, Ms. Hamilton
> studied winemaking for five years and apprenticed as a
> winemaker for Mr. Russell. When Ms. Hamilton came
> to work for Mr. Russell, Mr. Russell gave her an
> employee handbook, which indicated that he
> considered the partial short fermentation process to be
> confidential. Ms. Hamilton also knew that Mr. Russell
> had never disclosed his process to anyone else. She was
> the only person who knew of Mr. Russell's winemaking
> manual, which included details of the process. During
> the course of her employment, Ms. Hamilton was given
> access to the manual on two occasions to help revise the
> manual. During one of those occasions, Ms. Hamilton
> copied the manual.

But be careful with implied topic sentences. While implied topic sentences work really well in some types of writing, they're typically less effective in legal writing. Remember that readers, especially busy readers, understand information best if they are able to grasp its significance as soon as they see it. The more complex the information—and legal analysis is very complex—the more important it is for the reader to be able to grasp its significance quickly. The bottom line: the better the topic sentence, the more easily your reader is going to follow, understand, and retain the details in your paragraph.

2. Provide Transitions

Providing introductions is crucial for turning organized writing into coherent writing. But, while an introduction will help your reader get started, it won't always prevent her from stumbling along the way. Think of it this way: an introduction is a map. It tells the reader where she's going and how she will get there. But even the most adept traveler needs more than a map to get her where she's going. She also needs some road signs along the way to keep her pointed in the right direction. Without those road signs, she will lose confidence that she's headed in the right direction.

Two broad categories of transitions will help your reader feel confident that she's headed in the right direction. The first category—transitional words and phrases—are explicit transitions. They serve as clear road signs, helping your reader understand where she's at and where she's going. The transitions in the second category—substantive transitions—aren't as explicit as the first. They are a bit more like bridges on her route, but they will still build your reader's confidence in the direction she's headed.

Because transitions help your reader understand the relationships between what she has read and what she is about to read, these two categories of transitions work both between paragraphs and between sentences. When you use these transitions to help your reader see connections between paragraphs and connections between sentences, she will immediately know where she is and where she's going. The result is that she will experience your writing as organized.

✍ Editing Strategy 2.4
Check for Transitional Words and Phrases

To help your reader see the link between one idea and the next, you can sometimes simply choose a word or a phrase that represents the relationship between those two ideas. These transitional words and phrases quickly demonstrate the relationship between ideas and therefore create coherence.

Chart 2.4
Transitional Words and Phrases[3]

For Contrast

however	nevertheless	but
on the other hand	conversely	although

For Comparison

similarly	likewise	in the same way
for the same reason	by the same token	

For Cause and Effect

therefore	accordingly	hence
consequently	thus	since
as a result	so	because

For Addition

also	further	in addition
moreover	besides	too
and	additionally	as well

For Examples

for example	for instance	specifically

For Restatement

in other words	more simply	that is

For Time

subsequently	later	earlier
eventually	afterwards	meanwhile
initially	simultaneously	since

For Sequence

first, second, third	next	then
former, latter	final	later
in the first place	finally	primary, secondary

For Conclusion

in summary	in brief	in short
thus	therefore	consequently
finally	in conclusion	in review

These transitional words, because they tend to be rather generic, are sometimes the first to get cut in a writer's quest for brevity. But be careful

---

3. This list comes in large part from Anne Enquist & Laurel Currie Oates, *Just Writing: Grammar, Punctuation, and Style for the Legal Writer* 56-58 (4th ed. 2013).

not to sacrifice the clarity that these words can bring. Take, for instance, the sentences in Example 2.4(a). In the draft, the sentences are logically organized. But the reader has to work harder than she should have to in order to understand the logical relationship between the sentences. In the revision, the simple addition of a transitional word makes the relationship immediately clear and the writing coherent. The reader won't have to pause — even for a moment — to ponder the relationship that the writer intended to demonstrate.

Example 2.4(a)
Disjointed sentences revised by adding transitional word

Draft: The defendant in *Woodruff* made his attack repeatedly available to the public by posting his "Wanted" poster in the post office and local high school and showing it to a local citizen. Dixon made her three attacks repeatedly available to the public by posting them all to the internet and refusing to remove them.

Revision: The defendant in *Woodruff* made his attack repeatedly available to the public by posting his "Wanted" poster in the post office and local high school and showing it to a local citizen. **Similarly,** Dixon made her three attacks repeatedly available to the public by posting them all to the internet and refusing to remove them.

While the addition of the transition word in Example 2.4(a) is helpful, a reader wouldn't necessarily be lost without the transitional word. In part, that's because the writer has provided coherence by using parallel language.

However, there are times when omitting transitional words really will cause a reader to stumble. Take a look at Example 2.4(b). Without the guidance of the transition, the reader will struggle to determine whether the third sentence is a conclusion to the second or whether it is an addition. By adding transitional words, the writer has made the logical organization of these sentences, which is clear to him, clear to the reader.

Example 2.4(b)
Disjointed sentence revised by adding transitional words

Draft: Dixon's accusations were as derogatory as those in *Woodruff*. Accusing a person of sexual misdeeds, adultery, tax evasion, failure to pay child support, and being a "potentially violent" and "mentally unstable monster" is likely more offensive than disseminating a

30-year-old arrest record that arose out of a college prank. Dixon's attacks were just as persistent as the attacks in *Woodruff*.

Revision: **To begin**, Dixon's accusations were as derogatory as those in *Woodruff*. Accusing a person of sexual misdeeds, adultery, tax evasion, failure to pay child support, and being a "potentially violent" and "mentally unstable monster" is likely more offensive than disseminating a 30-year-old arrest record that arose out of a college prank. **Moreover**, Dixon's attacks were just as persistent as the attacks in *Woodruff*.

Transitional words and phrases can link paragraphs in the same way that they link sentences. The key to effectively transitioning between paragraphs is to remember that you are connecting ideas. This means that, typically, the transitional word should connect the first sentence (the topic sentence) of one paragraph to the first sentence of the next. This is exactly what happened with the addition of transitions in Example 2.4(c).

Example 2.4(c)
Disjointed paragraphs revised by adding transitional words

Draft: A claimant's use is open and notorious when the record owner actually knows of the claimant's possession of the land. *Vezey v. Green*, 35 P.3d 14, 22 (Alaska 2001). In *Vezey*, the owners had given the land in question to the claimant, repeatedly referred to it as belonging to the claimant, and refused to sell that land because it belonged to the claimant. *Id.* at 18. The court held that ...

A claimant can establish open and notorious use when her activities are sufficiently visible that a reasonably diligent owner should have had notice of her possession. *Nome 2000 v. Fagerstrom*, 799 P.2d 304, 309 (Alaska 1990). *In Nome 2000*, the claimants used a parcel of land in a semi-wilderness area to gather ...

Revision: A claimant's use is open and notorious when the record owner actually knows of the claimant's possession of the land. *Vezey v. Green*, 35 P.3d 14, 22 (Alaska 2001). In *Vezey*, the owners had given the land in question to the claimant, repeatedly referred to it as belonging to the claimant, and refused to sell that land because it

> belonged to the claimant. *Id.* at 18. The court held that …
>
> **As an alternative,** a claimant can **also** establish open and notorious use when her activities are sufficiently visible that a reasonably diligent owner should have had notice of her possession. *Nome 2000 v. Fagerstrom*, 799 P.2d 304, 309 (Alaska 1990). In *Nome 2000*, the claimants used a parcel of land in a semi-wilderness area to gather …

Again, the addition of the transitional word *also* in Example 2.4(c) is not as crucial as if the writer had been making a more substantial shift. In Example 2.4(d), the reader really would stumble pretty significantly without the transition.

Example 2.4(d)
Disjointed paragraph revised by adding transitional words

Draft: McLaughlin can also establish that Dixon's conduct was as extreme and outrageous as the store manager's conduct in *West*. In *West*, the store manager could foresee that his repeated attacks were likely to cause injury because he had been warned about the wife's poor health. Similarly, here, McLaughlin told Dixon in an e-mail that, as a result of her second posting, he was being harassed, that he could not sleep or eat, and that he worried he would lose an important client. Nevertheless, she kept her statement posted publicly on the internet and she added the final posting describing McLaughlin as a "monster." Assuming that her postings were as unwarranted as the store manager's attack was in *West*, a jury could also find that Dixon's conduct was extreme and outrageous because she persisted despite knowing the harm her statements were causing.

Dixon may argue that her postings were warranted. Dixon may argue that she acted out of a desire to warn the public about a dangerous man. She will likely rely on *Briggs* to argue that simply because her postings were unflattering does not mean that a jury could find they were extreme and outrageous. Rather, she will argue that her postings are an "honest, sincere" effort to describe a person and, therefore, they are insufficient to establish extreme and outrageous conduct.

Revision: McLaughlin can also establish that Dixon's conduct
              was as extreme and outrageous as the store manager's
              conduct in *West*. In *West*, the store manager could
              foresee that his repeated attacks were likely to cause
              injury because he had been warned about the wife's
              poor health. Similarly, here, McLaughlin told Dixon
              in an e-mail that, as a result of her second posting, he
              was being harassed, that he could not sleep or eat,
              and that he worried he would lose an important client.
              Nevertheless, she kept her statement posted publicly on
              the internet and she added the final posting describing
              McLaughlin as a "monster." Assuming that her postings
              were as unwarranted as the store manager's attack was
              in *West*, a jury could also find that Dixon's conduct was
              extreme and outrageous because she persisted despite
              knowing the harm her statements were causing.

              However, Dixon may argue that her postings were
              warranted. Dixon may argue that she acted out of a
              desire to warn the public about a dangerous man. She
              will likely rely on *Briggs* to argue that simply because her
              postings were unflattering does not mean that a jury
              could find they were extreme and outrageous. Rather,
              she will argue that her postings are an "honest, sincere"
              effort to describe a person and, therefore, they are
              insufficient to establish extreme and outrageous conduct.

By leading with a word of contrast, the writer cues to the reader that he's making a shift and allows the reader to make that shift at the same time. Without the word of contrast, the reader is going to have to go back and read the sentence again once she figures the shift out for herself. The result is that she won't experience the writing as organized.

First, Second, and Third: Sequence Words of Transition

Transition words that signal a sequence (first, second, third) made an appearance on the list of transitional words and phrases. But they're so important that they deserve another mention.

Words that signal sequence serve as transitions, but they also make really powerful road signs. For example, if your memo discusses four elements, labeling the elements — first, second, third, and fourth — will help your reader to immediately know where she's at in your analysis.

The trick to using these road signs is to start with a map (for example, there are two reasons that the lower court erred) and then use consistent language in each of the signposts (don't suddenly switch from reasons to issues or your reader will get lost).

The key to using these road signs is that you must have a *reason* to use them. Labeling things as first, second, and third where there's no logical reason to label them that way will only be confusing.

✍ Editing Strategy 2.5
Check for Substantive Transitions

Transitional words and phrases are helpful tools for creating coherence. But these kinds of explicit transitions aren't always necessary. In fact, using only explicit transitions would likely get repetitive and probably even a little dull.

Instead, you can use a substantive transition to create a bridge between what your reader has just read and what she's about to read. A substantive transition is pretty much what it sounds like. It serves both to give the reader substance and to transition the reader from one idea to another. Substantive transitions are often called dovetail transitions, which is also a pretty fitting name. Carpenters use dovetail joints to fasten wood without using nails or screws. They simply cut the two parts in a way that allows them to fit securely and seamlessly together. So, if transitional words are the nails that you see, then substantive transitions are the seamless fasteners that hold your writing together invisibly.

Example 2.5(a) demonstrates how a substantive transition both gives substance and transitions the reader.

Example 2.5(a)
Effective substantive transition

Revision: A jury could find Dixon's conduct to be extreme and outrageous. **Conduct** is **extreme and outrageous** when it goes "beyond all possible bounds of decency, and [is] regarded as atrocious, and utterly intolerable in a civilized community." *Briggs v. Rosenthal*, 327 S.E.2d 308, 311 (N.C. App. 1985).

In Example 2.5(a), the writer has created a substantive transition by repeating the word *conduct* and the phrase *extreme and outrageous* at the beginning of the second sentence. By repeating these words, the writer has both signaled the relationship between the two sentences (the second is going to further explain the first) and begun the substance of the second sentence. Notice, though, that the transition is effective only because it comes at the beginning of the second sentence to create a link between the two sentences. If the writer rearranged even a few words, as in Example 2.5(b), she would no longer have an effective transition.

Example 2.5(b)
Ineffective substantive transition

Draft: A jury could find Dixon's conduct to be extreme and outrageous. When conduct goes "beyond all possible bounds of decency, and [is] regarded as atrocious, and utterly intolerable in a civilized community," then it is extreme and outrageous. *Briggs v. Rosenthal*, 327 S.E.2d 308, 311 (N.C. App. 1985).

---

3. Creating Organization Before Coherence

All of the approaches to creating coherence in your writing in this chapter assume that your writing already has a logical organization. If you find that you are struggling, for example, to create a substantive transition between two sentences, you may need to take a step back. You may need to decide if what you're really struggling to do is find a logical connection between those two sentences. Doing this—creating a logical order to your writing—is a much more difficult task than turning organized writing into coherent writing. But you may discover that, as you edit to be sure that your writing is coherent, you are forced to think deeply about the underlying organization of your writing. By doing this, though, you'll be doing yourself and your busy reader a favor.

Coherent Writing:
The Exercises

The following text appears in a memo about burglary. Underline and label any introductions, topic sentences, or transitional words that help create the memo's coherence.

The mobile bakery that Justin Dennison broke into is a building under Oregon burglary law. The State can establish that a structure is a building in one of two ways: (1) by proving that the structure is a "building" in the "ordinary meaning" of that term or (2) by proving that it is a "booth, vehicle, boat, aircraft, or other structure adapted for overnight accommodation of persons or for carrying on business therein." Or. Rev. Stat. § 164.205(1) (2013). Because the van is not a building within the ordinary meaning of that term, the question is whether it is a vehicle adapted for overnight accommodation of persons or for carrying on business therein.

While the van is occasionally used as a place of overnight accommodation, it has not been sufficiently adapted for overnight accommodation under the statute. However, it has been adapted for carrying on business. A vehicle is adapted if it is changed or modified so that it is suitable for a new or different use. *State v. Nollen*, 196 P.3d 788, 789 (Or. App. 2004). This new or different use must be a business use, which is simply "'a commercial or industrial enterprise.'" *Id.* (*quoting* Webster's Third New Int'l Dictionary 23 (unabridged ed. 1993)).

In *Nollen*, the court held that a semi-truck trailer was a building because it had been adapted for use as a business. *Id.* St. Vincent de Paul, a charitable organization, used the semi-truck trailer as a donation center. *Id.* at 788. A truck would tow a trailer to the transfer station, but then the driver would detach the trailer and leave it for a period of time. *Id*. In addition to the driver leaving the trailer for a period of time, St. Vincent placed a temporary stairway next to the trailer so that members of the public could walk up the stairs and into the trailer to make their donations. *Id*. St. Vincent also placed permanent signs near the trailer advertising it as a donation collection station. *Id*. According to the court, by making these changes, St. Vincent had adapted the trailer from its ordinary use as a vehicle to use in the business of collecting and redistributing donations. *Id*. at 789. The court reasoned that, because the statute does not require that the adaptation of a vehicle be permanent, the changes to the trailer were sufficient even though the trailer was not permanently located at the transfer station. *Id*. Thus, the trailer was a building. *Id*.

On the other hand, in *State v. Scott*, 590 P.2d 743, 744 (Or. App. 1979), the court held that a railroad boxcar was not a building because it had not been modified to be used as anything other than a vehicle. In *Scott*, the defendant entered a railroad boxcar with the intent to commit a crime. *See id*. However, because the railroad boxcar was not a building, the court overturned the defendant's burglary conviction. *Id*. The court noted that a boxcar could conceivably be adapted for business. *Id*. However, because the boxcar in that case had not been changed in any way from its ordinary purpose—that is, because it was still simply a "structure on wheels designed for the storage of goods and their transportation"—the court held that it was not a building. *Id*.

Here, the mobile bakery that Mr. Dennison entered is a building because it has been adapted for carrying on business. The mobile bakery, which was originally simply a utility van, has been changed and modified, much in the same way that the trailer in *Nollen* was modified and stands in contrast to the boxcar in *Scott*. Like the trailer in *Nollen*, which was detached from the truck that towed it, the van's awning was open and extending from the side of the van and chairs were positioned under that awning. These changes make both the trailer in *Nollen* and the mobile bakery unsuitable for use as a vehicle while they are in business. But Ms. Carlson has made even more changes to the van, which make it markedly different from the boxcar in *Scott*. Unlike in *Scott*, where there was no evidence that the boxcar had been modified at all, there is ample evidence of modifications to the van. Ms. Carlson put down laminate flooring and added refrigerator space for her products and added a sink and small bathroom. All of these changes demonstrate that the van has been adapted for a new purpose.

Moreover, the changes to the mobile bakery make it suitable for use in a commercial or industrial enterprise. In other words, the van, like the truck in *Nollen* but unlike the boxcar in *Scott*, is suitable for use as a business. Just like St. Vincent, which placed stairs next to the donation truck so that patrons could enter the trailer and leave their donations, Ms. Carlson opens the van doors and the side window to create a service counter, and she opens the awning at the side of the van so that patrons can relax in chairs in its shade. In addition, like St. Vincent advertising the trailer as the location of its business, Ms. Carlson advertises the mobile bakery as the location of her business. St. Vincent de Paul placed permanent signs near the trailer advertising it as a donation center. While Ms. Carlson has no permanent signs to advertise her van as a mobile bakery, she does display signs listing the cupcake flavors and prices, and she plays music from a portable speaker. Both the temporary cupcake signs and the music serve a similar purpose to St. Vincent's permanent signs—advertising a business. In fact, the changes that Ms. Carlson made to the van are presumably the kinds of changes that the court in *Scott* alluded to when it suggested that a vehicle could conceivably be modified so that it could be used for business purposes. Ms. Carlson's van is now much more than just a "structure on wheels designed for the storage of goods and their transportation." Through the changes, it has become suitable for use as a business and thus is a building. Unlike the lack of changes to the railroad boxcar in *Scott* and like the changes to the trailer in *Nollen*, the changes to the mobile bakery adapted the vehicle from its ordinary use for transportation to use in Ms. Carlson's bakery business.

However, Mr. Dennison may argue that the changes Ms. Carlson made to the mobile cupcake van were not as significant as the changes made to the trailer in *Nollen*. He may argue that, unlike the detached trailer in *Nollen*, the van really continued to be a vehicle. However, because there is no statutory requirement that the adaptation of the vehicle be permanent, this argument is unlikely to succeed. Even though the van might have occasionally been simply transportation like the railroad car in *Scott*, while it was parked and doing business as a mobile bakery, it was a building.

Chapter 3

Vigorous Writing

"Vigorous writing is concise. A sentence should contain no unnecessary words, a paragraph no unnecessary sentences, for the same reason that a drawing should have no unnecessary lines and a machine no unnecessary parts." — William Strunk, Jr.

A lot of legal writing is hard to read. Some of it is difficult to read because the concepts and ideas are difficult. But just as often, legal writing is hard to read because it lacks vigor. It sits stagnant on the page, and only through sheer force of will can you make your way through the muck to understand what is important.

Vigorous writing, on the other hand, is dynamic. It jumps off the page and can pull even a reluctant reader along with it. Vigorous writing pulls readers along by using just the right words to create mental pictures. Those pictures help the reader stay engaged with even the most difficult ideas. Vigorous writing is also stripped down to its essentials. Truly dynamic writing doesn't force readers to wade through ten words when only two are necessary.

Choosing just the right words and stripping your writing down to its essentials are not writing tasks—they are rewriting tasks. Trying to choose just the right word as you first get your thoughts down on paper is likely to stifle your creativity. And it will definitely slow you down. So, save these tasks, and, once you have that first draft, go back and revise. To make sure that you have chosen the right words to create clear mental pictures, look at each sentence and ask yourself whether it has a concrete subject and a strong, active verb. To strip your writing to its essentials, write short, uncluttered sentences and omit surplus words. Once you have chosen just the right words and stripped your writing to its essentials, you might discover that your writing is beginning to jump off the page.

Vigorous Writing:
The Editing Checklist

1. Use Concrete Subjects and Strong, Active Verbs

✍ 3.1 Check for Abstract Nouns at the Beginning of a Sentence

Use your computer's find function to search for empty abstract nouns at the beginning of a sentence. Delete them.

✍ 3.2 Check for *It is* and *There are* at the Beginning of a Sentence

Use your computer's find function to search for *it is* and *there are*. Delete these whenever they appear at the beginning of a sentence.

✍ 3.3 Check for Vague Verbs

Replace vague verbs with strong, active verbs.

✍ 3.4 Check for Passive Voice

To find the passive voice, search for any form of the verb *be*. When you find it, look to see whether it is followed by a verb ending in *-d, -ed, -n, -en,* or *-t*. If you see these verbs together, the actor in the sentence is probably receiving the action instead of doing it. Revise the sentence so that the actor is doing the action.

✍ 3.5 Check for Nominalizations

To find nominalizations, search for words ending in *-ion* or *-ment*. These words are often paired with the word *of* and signal that a verb has become a noun. Turn that noun back into a verb.

2. Write Uncluttered Sentences

✍ 3.6 Check for Long Sentences

Look for sentences that are longer than two lines. If a sentence is longer than two lines, use your word processor to do a word count. If the sentence is longer than 25 words, consider shortening it.

✍ 3.7 Check for Too Many Independent Clauses in a Single Sentence

Look for sentences that are really made up of several independent clauses. Consider making the individual independent clauses into sentences.

✍ 3.8 Check for Too Many Dependent Clauses in a Single Sentence

Look for sentences that are really made up of several dependent clauses. Consider making the information in the dependent clause its own sentence or, if it's not crucial information, consider deleting it altogether.

✍ 3.9 Check for Too Many Prepositional Phrases in a Single Sentence

Look for sentences with too many prepositions. Where you see too many prepositions in one sentence, chances are that the sentence has too many prepositional phrases. Either omit some of the prepositional phrases or change their form.

3. Omit Surplus Words

✍ 3.10 Check for Wordy Phrases

Look for phrases that could be replaced by a word or two. Replace them.

4. Combining Vigor and Variety

Vigorous Writing:
The Details

1. Use Concrete Subjects and Strong, Active Verbs

Grammar Reminder

The **subject** of a sentence names who or what the sentence is about. The subject of a sentence is, often, everything that comes before the verb. So, if you're having trouble finding the subject, switch tactics and look for the verb.

Readers intuitively look for the subject and verb of each sentence. They want to know who is doing what. In fact, to be complete, every English sentence must contain a SUBJECT and a VERB. As a result, the subject and the verb are the parts of the sentence that are most important to creating a mental picture for your reader. You will create the clearest picture—and thus the most vigorous writing—if you use a concrete NOUN as your subject and a strong, active verb.

Grammar Reminder

A **verb** is a word that expresses action or being.

> ✎ Editing Strategy 3.1
> ### Check for Abstract Nouns at the Beginning of a Sentence

Grammar Reminder

A **noun** is a word that names a person, place, or thing.

Most of us know what a noun is—it is a person, place, or thing. But many of us do not give much thought to the difference between a specific, concrete noun and an abstract noun. A concrete noun is, most often, a person, a place, or a physical object (think: judge, defendant, court, written judicial opinion). An abstract noun, on the other hand, is, most often, an idea or concept (think: liability, negligence, reasonableness). The difference is significant because specific, concrete nouns create clear pictures. Abstract nouns, on the other hand, are just harder for your reader to visualize. A sentence with an abstract subject will slow your reader down, and your writing will lose some of its vigor.

Using a concrete subject seems like an easy thing to do. But what seems simple in theory is actually much more difficult in practice. In legal writing, abstract nouns are quite common because lawyers often deal in ideas and concepts. More often than not, we are thinking and writing about liability, negligence, and tests.

But you can and should edit out at least some of the abstract nouns in your writing. To edit out abstract nouns, start by finding the GRAMMATICAL SUBJECT of your sentence and decide whether it is an idea or concept rather than a person or object. If it is an idea or concept, it is an abstract noun. Next, decide whether you can replace the idea or concept with a person or object. If you can, you should.

What Is a Grammatical Subject? And Why Does It Matter?

A sentence's grammatical subject is, essentially, the noun or noun phrase at the beginning of the sentence. For example, in the sentence "The defendant was convicted by the jury," the grammatical subject is the defendant.

But, in that sentence, the defendant is not actually *doing* anything. In fact, the jury is doing the action. The jury is *convicting*. So the jury is the real subject — the *logical subject* — of the sentence.

Your sentences will be much easier to read and much more vigorous if you make sure that the logical subject of your sentence is also the grammatical subject of your sentence. So, in the earlier example, the sentence would become "The jury convicted the defendant."

In Example 3.1(a), the writer could replace the abstract noun — *second-degree burglary* — with a concrete noun — *a person*. Even though *person* is a relatively generic noun, it is still much more concrete than the abstract concept of burglary and makes the sentence more vigorous.

Example 3.1(a)
Sentence revised by replacing abstract noun with concrete noun

Draft: Second-degree burglary requires "enter[ing] or remain[ing] unlawfully in a building with the intent to commit a crime." Or. Rev. Stat. § 164.215(1) (2013).

Revision: A **person** commits second-degree burglary if she "enters or remains unlawfully in a building with the intent to commit a crime." Or. Rev. Stat. § 164.215(1) (2013).

In Example 3.1(b), on the other hand, the writer decided that it was best to keep the abstract noun — *second-degree burglary* — as the subject of the second sentence. But she was thoughtful about this revision. She decided that she could risk an abstract noun because (1) the first sentence begins with a concrete noun and (2) using an abstract noun in the second sentence provided a nice transition from the first sentence (for more on transitions, see Editing Strategies 2.4 and 2.5).

Example 3.1(b)
Abstract noun used effectively in a sentence

Draft: A person commits second-degree burglary if she "enters or remains unlawfully in a building with intent to commit a crime." Or. Rev. Stat. § 164.215(1) (2013). **Second-degree burglary** is elevated to first-degree burglary "if the

> building is a dwelling" or if the suspect possessed a
> burglary tool in the course of the burglary. *Id.*

Ultimately, your goal is not to make sure that *every* sentence begins with a concrete noun. Complete uniformity might get dull. Instead, your goal is to make sure that your writing, as a whole, is vigorous. So aim for making sure that *most* sentences begin with concrete nouns.

Even if you decide (thoughtfully, of course) to use an abstract noun as the subject of your sentence, some abstract nouns should be purged from your writing altogether. For lack of a better term, we will call these "empty abstract nouns." Look at Chart 3.1(1) for a list of some empty abstract nouns. You will see that these empty abstract nouns are words that are, well, empty. They don't mean anything, and they don't add anything to your writing.

Chart 3.1
Empty Abstract Nouns

nature of	kind of	type of
aspect of	factor of	area of
use of		

Earlier, in Example 3.1(b), the noun—*second-degree burglary*—was abstract, but it also had meaning. Compare that abstract noun with the list of nouns in Chart 3.1(1). The abstract nouns in that list do not really mean anything at all.

To see one of these "empty abstract nouns" in a sentence, take a look at Example 3.1(c). The draft sentence contains an empty abstract noun—*the type of*. In her first revision, the writer simply purged that empty abstract noun. In her second revision, the writer went even farther and replaced the abstract *test* with the concrete *courts*. The result is a more vigorous sentence.

Example 3.1(c)
Sentence revised by replacing empty abstract noun with concrete noun

Draft: **The type of test** a court will use to determine liability depends on the particular circumstances of the situation.

First Revision: **The test** a court will use to determine liability depends on the particular circumstances of the situation.

Second Revision:	**Courts** use different tests to determine liability in different situations.

Even if you decide to leave an abstract noun in place (as in the first revision in Example 3.1(c)), you should still get rid of any empty abstract nouns. For instance, in Example 3.1(d), the revised version still begins with an abstract noun—*family structures*—but the writer eliminated the clutter around it—*the very nature of.*

Example 3.1(d)
Sentence revised by replacing empty abstract noun with abstract noun

Draft:	**The very nature of family structures** has changed dramatically over the last decade.
Revision:	**Family structures** have changed dramatically over the last decade.

The good news is that finding those empty abstract nouns is simple: use your computer's find function to search for the abstract phrases in Chart 3.1(1). When you find a sentence that begins with an empty abstract noun, get rid of it. You are likely to discover that you quickly commit the list to memory. And once you get over your attachment to the lawyerly sound of these phrases, you will probably purge them from your writing altogether.

✐ Editing Strategy 3.2
Check for *It is* and *There are* at the Beginning of a Sentence

An abstract noun at the beginning of your sentence is a sign that you are not using a concrete subject. A related mistake is using *it is* or *there are* at the beginning of a sentence, which is a sign that you are just delaying the subject. While you may have a concrete subject in your sentence, you are making your reader wait for it, which is almost as bad as not including it at all. In some situations, delaying the subject might serve to draw additional attention to the subject; however, most of the time, beginning a sentence with *it is* or *there are* just slows down your writing.

Luckily, finding and fixing this problem is easy. Again, use your computer's find function and search for *it is* and *there are*. When you see an *it is* or a *there are* at the beginning of a sentence, get rid of it. Examples 3.2(a) and 3.2(b) show how easily you can purge these extra words from your sentences.

Example 3.2(a)
Sentence revised by removing *it is* from the beginning of the sentence

Draft: **It is** likely that a court would hold that Officer Dennis seized Young when she kept his license to run a warrants check.

Revision: **A court** would likely hold that Officer Dennis seized Young when she kept his license to run a warrants check.

Example 3.2(b)
Sentence revised by removing *there are* from the beginning of the sentence

Draft: **There are** several circumstances that might indicate that a seizure has occurred.

Revision: **Several circumstances** might indicate that a seizure has occurred.

✍ Editing Strategy 3.3
Check for Vague Verbs

Just as most of us know what a noun is, most of us also know what a verb is: it is a word that expresses action. Of course, verbs are more complicated than that. They are not always just a single word and they do not always express action. (Sometimes they express a state of being: *is, become.*) And not all verbs are created equal: some are specific while others are quite vague. While you can get along pretty well as a writer without knowing all of the complexities of verbs, you will likely find it very difficult to write vigorously until you can spot vague verbs.

To understand what a vague verb is, consider the following sentence: *The girl exercised.* The verb—*exercised*—expresses action, but it is also pretty vague. What, exactly, was the girl doing? Swimming? Lifting weights? Taking a yoga class? A more specific verb will create a clearer, more accurate picture.

Just as abstract nouns are common in legal writing, vague verbs tend to show up quite a bit as well. The term vague verb is difficult to define, however, because a vague verb is any verb that really could be more specific. Think of the difference between *exercise* and *swim*. The verb *exercise* is vague simply because it could be more specific—*swim*. When it comes to verbs, then, a good rule of thumb is that if your verb could be more specific, it should be more specific.

While it is important to understand the difference between a vague verb and a specific verb, vague verbs can sometimes be difficult to spot— especially in legal writing. After all, in a complicated legal analysis, the difference between a vague verb and a specific verb probably will not be as obvious as the difference between *exercise* and *swim*.

To get you started, Chart 3.3(1) lists some vague verbs that tend to show up frequently in legal writing.

Chart 3.3
Vague Verbs

concerns	reveals
involves	deals with
discusses	to be

When you find one of these vague verbs, just as when you find an abstract noun, get rid of it. With a vague verb, however, you have to do more than just get rid of it. You have to replace it with another verb. Finding a new verb will require you to think about what you are actually trying to say. Although deciding what you are trying to say may take some work, the work will be worth it; you will begin thinking—and writing—more precisely and vividly.

Take a look at Example 3.3(a). The verb starts out vague—*deals with*. From a reader's perspective, *deals with* means almost nothing. So the writer revises to use a more specific verb. Then the writer revises again so that the logical subject of the sentence—*the parties*—is also the grammatical subject of the sentence.

Example 3.3(a)
Sentence revised by replacing vague verb with a more specific verb

Draft:	Paragraph 17 of the contract **deals with** notice.
Revision:	Paragraph 17 of the contract **requires** the parties to give 15 days advance notice of any delay.
Second Revision:	According to Paragraph 17 of the contract, the parties **must give** each other 15 days advance notice of any delays.

Editing Strategy 3.4
Check for Passive Voice

While you can first comb through your writing looking for abstract subjects and then do a separate edit looking for vague verbs, you will often find that these enemies of vigor are working in tandem. The PASSIVE VOICE is a perfect example of an abstract subject-vague verb combination.

Passive voice is a sure sign that you are not using a concrete subject. In fact, one defining characteristic of the passive voice is that it takes the actor (otherwise known as the concrete noun) out of the grammatical subject and sticks it in a PREPOSITIONAL PHRASE, or, even worse, eliminates it from the sentence altogether. Example 3.4(a) shows how the writer took the actor — *the jury foreman* — out of the subject and put her in a prepositional phrase at the end of the sentence.

> **Example 3.4(a)**
> **Passive voice sentence with the actor/logical subject in a prepositional phrase**
> Draft: The deliberations are run by the jury foreman.

In addition to beginning a sentence with an abstract subject, the passive voice also requires you to use a wordy verb. In sentences written in the passive voice, the verb will consist of a form of the verb *be* (*be, am, is, are, was, were, being, been*) and a PAST PARTICIPLE (a verb ending in *-d, -ed, -n, -en,* or *-t*). This two-word verb is, well, one more word that you need.

That unnecessarily long two-word verb will also help you find sentences written in the passive voice. Begin your search for the passive by looking for the *be* verb. When you find it, look to see whether it is followed by a verb ending in *-d, -ed, -n, -en,* or *-t*. This second step is important because, unless the *be* verb is paired with a past participle, it is not a signal of the passive voice. Take, for instance, the sentence in Example 3.4(b). The *be* verb is there, but it is paired with an *-ing* verb (also known as a **present participle**), not a past participle. So, it is not a signal of the passive voice.

> **Example 3.4(b)**
> **Sentence with a *be* verb that does not signal the passive voice**
> Draft: The jury foreman **was running** the deliberations.

But when you discover a *be* verb that is paired with a past participle, check to see whether the actor in the sentence is receiving the action instead of doing it. Example 3.4(c) lists several sentences where the *be* verb is paired with a past participle. In the first, the real actor in the sentence is receiving the action. In the last three, the real actor has been omitted altogether.

> **Example 3.4(c)**
> **Sentences written in the passive voice**
>
> Draft: The deliberations **are run** by the jury foreman.
>
> Draft: The defendant **was found** guilty.
>
> Draft: The case **was remanded** to the trial court.
>
> Draft: Too much time **had been spent** reviewing the trial transcript.

After identifying a sentence written in the passive voice, fix it by putting the actor into the grammatical subject of the sentence. To put the actor (the logical subject) in the grammatical subject of the sentence, you may just need to move the actor from one part of the sentence to another, as in Example 3.4(d).

> **Example 3.4(d)**
> **Passive voice sentence revised by making the logical subject the grammatical subject**
>
> Draft: The deliberations are run by **the jury foreman**.
>
> Revision: **The jury foreman** runs the deliberations.

But if the sentence has been written in the TRUNCATED PASSIVE VOICE — if the actor of the sentence has been omitted from the sentence altogether — you will actually have to rewrite the sentence to include the actor, as in Example 3.4(e).

Grammar Reminder

Sentences written in the passive voice often hide the logical subject of the sentence in a prepositional phrase. Sentences written in the **truncated passive voice** omit the prepositional phrase with the logical subject altogether.

> **Example 3.4(e)**
> **Passive voice sentences revised by supplying the logical subject and making it the grammatical subject**
>
> Draft: The defendant **was found** guilty.
>
> Revision: The jury found the defendant guilty.
>
> Draft: The case **was remanded** to the trial court.
>
> Revision: The appellate court remanded the case to the trial court.
>
> Draft: Too much time **had been spent** reviewing the trial transcript.
>
> Revision: The associate had spent too much time reviewing the trial transcript.

Because the passive voice affects the vigor of your writing, you should know how to find it and fix it. But you do not always need to purge the passive from your writing.

The passive voice is appropriate in several circumstances. First, if you do not know who the real actor is, as in Example 3.4(f), you will have almost no choice but to use the passive voice.

Example 3.4(f)
Passive voice used effectively

Revision: The bank **was robbed**.

The passive voice is also appropriate where the person performing the action is relatively unimportant. In Example 3.4(g), the identity of the officers who arrested the defendant is not important.

Example 3.4(g)
Passive voice used effectively

Revision: The defendant **was arrested** near the scene of the crime.

Finally, the passive voice can be effective if you want to emphasize the action rather than the actor. While Example 3.4(h) could have been written with "the jury" as the subject, the writer chose to emphasize the action of conviction.

Example 3.4(h)
Passive voice used effectively

Revision: The defendant **was convicted** of first-degree burglary.

✍ Editing Strategy 3.5
Check for Nominalizations

Grammar Reminder
A **nominalization** is a verb that is functioning as a noun.

NOMINALIZATIONS also indicate a weak subject-verb combination. In a nominalization, the verb—e.g., *participate*—becomes a noun—e.g., *participation*—and the real noun can be omitted from the sentence altogether. For instance, read the first sentence in Example 3.5(a). You will see that the verb—*take*—became a noun—*the taking of*. Then, if you look at the revision, it becomes even clearer that the real noun in the sentence—*the officer*—was actually omitted altogether. You can see, then, that if the most vigorous sentences begin with a concrete noun and a strong, active verb, nominalizations can cause real trouble.

Example 3.5(a)
Sentences with nominalizations revised by turning the nominalization back into a verb and supplying a subject

Draft: The **taking of** the defendant's license was a seizure under the Fourth Amendment.

Revision: When the officer **took** the defendant's license, he seized the defendant for purposes of the Fourth Amendment.

Draft: The **rejection of** the defendant's argument was clear.

Revision: The jury clearly **rejected** the defendant's argument.

Nominalizations are particularly troublesome because they are hard to find. Like the passive voice, nominalizations are grammatically correct. So, they probably won't stand out to you as you are editing. To find nominalizations in your writing, you can look for the elements that often show up in a nominalization:

(1) an introductory word, such as *a, an, the, his, her, these,* or *several*;
(2) a verb functioning as a noun (a shortcut for finding a verb functioning as a noun: they usually end in *-ion, -ing,* or *-ment*); and
(3) the word *of*

Where you see all three of these things together, as in Example 3.5(b), you can almost be sure that you have found a nominalization.

Example 3.5(b)
Nominalization with all three elements revised by turning the nominalization back into a verb

Draft: The **establishment of** open and notorious, exclusive, hostile, and continuous possession of the property is necessary.

Revision: The claimants must **establish** that they had open and notorious, exclusive, hostile, and continuous possession of the property.

Some nominalizations, such as the nominalization in Example 3.5(c) will have just two elements.

Example 3.5(c)
Nominalization with two elements revised by turning the nominalization back into a verb

Draft: **Awarding of** attorneys fees is done on a case-by-case basis.

Revision: Judges **award** attorneys fees on a case-by-case basis.

All nominalizations will, at a minimum, have a verb that is acting like a noun. Example 3.5(d) demonstrates a nominalization with just a single element.

Example 3.5(d)
Nominalization with single element revised by turning the nominalization back into a verb

Draft: There were many **indications** that the defendant had been involved in the burglary.

Revision: The evidence **indicated** that the defendant had been involved in the burglary.

Because all nominalizations have a verb that is actually functioning as a noun, the key to finding a nominalization is to look for words that end in *-ion, -ing* or *-ment*. Often, as in Examples 3.5(b), 3.5(c), and 3.5(d), you will find that these words are nominalizations. While you won't catch all of the nominalizations in your writing this way, you will find many.

Once you find a nominalization, editing the nominalization is simple. To edit a nominalization, just turn the noun back into a verb, as in Example 3.5(e). Often, you may also need to insert an actual noun (preferably, a concrete one) and you may have to do a little rearranging.

Example 3.5(e)
Nominalization revised by turning the nominalization into a verb

Draft: **A conclusion** was made by the court that each of the individual, self-contained storage units was a building.

Revision: The court **concluded** that each of the individual, self-contained storage units was a building.

Like the passive voice, nominalizations aren't all bad, and you may decide to keep a nominalization. For example, you might retain a nominalization if you don't know who is doing the action or if the subject is unimportant. Also, if the nominalization comes from a statute, you might want to retain that nominalization when the exact statutory language is important. You just need to be sure that you can identify the nominalization and then justify using it.

When Editing Strategies Compete

Sometimes, editing strategies will compete. For instance, editing out a nominalization (Editing Strategy 3.5) will sometimes result in a longer sentence (Editing Strategy 3.6). In the first sentence in Example 3.5(a), the revised sentence is actually longer than the original sentence.

So, what do you do when editing strategies compete? You will have to decide which editing strategy makes the most sense under the circumstances. While the revised sentence in Example 3.5(a) is longer, it also creates a much clearer mental picture than the draft sentence. Thus, using Editing Strategy 3.5 under the circumstances made the most sense.

But before you choose one strategy over another, consider the possibility that two or more strategies could work together.

---

2. Write Uncluttered Sentences

When you have written sentences that use concrete subjects and strong, active verbs, you next need to review those sentences to determine whether they are stripped to their essentials. Once you have created clear pictures for your reader, you don't want those pictures blurred by a bunch of clutter.

Sentences can be cluttered for different reasons. Sometimes, sentences are cluttered because they have too many different ideas in them. In that case, the ideas just need to be separated. Other times sentences are cluttered because they have too much unnecessary information in them. In that case, you really just have to dump the clutter. No matter what the reason, though, de-cluttering your sentences is an important step in creating vigorous writing.

The easiest first step in de-cluttering your sentences is finding and revising long sentences. Long sentences, in and of themselves, are not always a problem. But long sentences do seem to be a gateway to cluttered sentences: the longer the sentence, the greater the likelihood that it is cluttered.

Then, to really be sure that you have de-cluttered, you should (1) check for too many INDEPENDENT CLAUSES, (2) check for too many DEPENDENT CLAUSES, and (3) check for too many prepositional phrases.

> **Grammar Reminder**
>
> An **independent clause** is a full sentence pattern — in other words, it has everything it needs to be a sentence — and it either stands alone as a sentence or *could* stand alone as a sentence.

> **Grammar Reminder**
>
> A **dependent clause**, like an independent clause, has everything it needs to be a sentence (a subject and a verb). But a dependent clause, unlike an independent clause, is linked to the rest of the sentence in a way that makes it depend on the rest of the sentence for its meaning. In other words, it can't stand alone.

✍ Editing Strategy 3.6
Check for Long Sentences

Usually, a reader struggles to absorb more than 25 words in a single sentence. If your sentences are consistently longer than 25 words, then your sentences are probably cluttered.

You can check for long sentences by scanning the page looking for sentences that are longer than two lines. If a sentence is longer than two lines, use your word processor to do a word count. If that word count is higher than 25, consider editing the sentence.

Editing a sentence that is too long is relatively easy. Simply turn the single long sentence into two or more shorter sentences. You can do this by looking for discrete ideas within the long sentence and giving each its own sentence, as in Example 3.6(a).

Example 3.6(a)
Long sentence revised by creating multiple short sentences

Draft: In the absence of an arrest warrant, an arrest must be based on probable cause, but a person may be temporarily detained, or seized, on less than probable cause if the police have a reasonable suspicion that the person stopped is engaged in criminal activity. *U.S. v. Lopez*, 443 F.3d 1280, 1283 (10th Cir. 2006).

Revision: In the absence of an arrest warrant, an arrest must be based on probable cause. *U.S. v. Lopez*, 443 F.3d 1280, 1283 (10th Cir. 2006). However, a person may be temporarily detained, or seized, on less than probable cause. *Id.* To justify a temporary seizure, the police must have a reasonable suspicion that the person stopped is engaged in criminal activity. *Id.*

If turning the long sentence into several shorter sentences does not make sense, find another way to give your reader a mental break. For example, numbering items in a list works well. This technique, illustrated in Example 3.6(b), is especially helpful when you are listing elements.

Example 3.6(b)
Long sentence revised by breaking up the length with a numbered list

Draft: To convince this Court that the district court improperly denied his motion to suppress, Mr. Young must demonstrate that Officer Dennis seized him when she retained his identification to run a warrants check and that Officer Dennis's discovery of an outstanding warrant did not purge the taint of the illegal seizure.

Revision: To convince this Court that the district court improperly denied his motion to suppress, Mr. Young must demonstrate that (1) Officer Dennis seized him when she retained his identification to run a warrants check and (2) Officer Dennis's discovery of an outstanding warrant did not purge the taint of the illegal seizure.

Sentences, Phrases, and Clauses, Oh My!

You can probably get by most of the time without knowing the difference between a clause and a phrase, but knowing the difference can be really helpful when it comes to writing vigorously or (maybe more importantly) punctuating correctly. So it probably makes sense to take a minute to understand the difference.

Clauses look just like sentences. They have subjects and verbs. In fact, independent clauses *are* sentences. Dependent clauses, like independent clauses, *look* just like sentences. The only difference is that a dependent clause doesn't *act* like a sentence. Instead, it fits inside a sentence and functions as an adjective, adverb, or noun.

Phrases, on the other hand, don't look or act like sentences. Phrases are just any group of at least two words that are linked together but don't have a subject and a verb. Phrases come in lots of different shapes and sizes — noun phrases (*the law school*), prepositional phrases (*in class*). They also function in lots of different ways. The bottom line is that they don't have both a subject and a verb and therefore are not clauses.

✍ Editing Strategy 3.7
Check for Too Many Independent Clauses in a Single Sentence

Once you have shorter sentences, de-clutter them. While shortening long sentences may have had the added bonus of cleaning up some clutter, even short sentences can be cluttered.

To start de-cluttering, find sentences that have multiple ideas nested in them. To find sentences with too many nested ideas, check for sentences that are made up of multiple independent clauses.

Searching for sentences with multiple independent clauses is actually straightforward. Simply remember that an independent clause is a full sentence. In other words, if a part of the sentence could actually *be* a sentence, then that part is an independent clause. In the draft sentence in Example 3.7(a), a single sentence is actually made up of two sentences hooked together with the word *and*. When sentences are hooked together like that, they are independent clauses.

Example 3.7(a)
Sentence with two independent clauses revised by creating two separate sentences

Draft: The St. Vincent de Paul Society placed a temporary stairway next to the trailer, **and** it also placed permanent signs near the trailer advertising it as a donation collection station. *State v. Nollen*, 100 P.3d 788, 788 (Or. App. 2004).

Revision: The St. Vincent de Paul Society placed a temporary stairway next to the trailer. *State v. Nollen*, 100 P.3d 788, 788 (Or. App. 2004). **It also** placed permanent signs near the trailer advertising it as a donation collection station. *Id.*

Grammar Reminder

A **conjunction** is a word used to join words, phrases, or clauses. Different kinds of conjunctions express different relationships between the words, phrases, or clauses that they join.

Coordinating conjunctions simply hook together two equal grammatical elements—two words, two phrases, or two clauses.

Finding independent clauses becomes even easier when you realize that, to join multiple independent clauses together as a sentence, you must often use a comma and a COORDINATING CONJUNCTION. Luckily, the list of coordinating conjunctions is short; they are all listed in Chart 3.7(1). (Fans of acronyms remember this list as the FANBOYS.)

Chart 3.7
Coordinating Conjunctions

for	and	nor	but	or	yet	so

So, to find sentences cluttered with too many ideas, begin by searching for coordinating conjunctions. If those coordinating conjunctions link together multiple independent clauses—that is, ideas that are really full sentences—consider whether revising might be necessary. The solution here is the same as it was for fixing an overly long sentence: give each independent clause its own sentence, as in Example 3.7(b). (You'll notice that the coordinating conjunctions are in bold.)

Example 3.7(b)
Sentence with too many independent clauses joined by too many coordinating conjunctions, revised by creating several sentences

Draft: The testimony established that the officers did not use flashing lights or sirens when they drove up to the men, **and** the officers did not block the men in or physically prevent them from leaving, **and** the officers did not display their weapons, **and** Officer Dennis spoke to the defendant in a calm voice, **and** she did not make physical contact with him prior to the arrest.

Revision: The testimony established that the officers did not use flashing lights or sirens when they drove up to the men. The officers did not block the men in, physically prevent them from leaving, or display their weapons. Officer Dennis spoke to the defendant in a calm voice and did not make physical contact with him prior to the arrest.

You don't need to give every independent clause its own sentence. In fact, doing that would actually result in fairly choppy writing. But you do need to consider the effect that multiple clauses, with multiple ideas, within a single sentence will have on your reader. If the ideas are important or complex enough, they need their own sentences. Forcing your reader to absorb three or four different ideas before she gets a break is going to frustrate her. It will slow her down and, as a result, your writing will lose its vigor.

Editing Strategy 3.8
Check for Too Many Dependent Clauses in a Single Sentence

Several independent clauses in a single sentence can be problematic but not nearly as problematic as several dependent clauses. The problem with dependent clauses is that they tend to nest inside of each other and tangle up your reader. Example 3.8(a) is an extreme, but not completely unrealistic, example. In that example, in order to illustrate the dependent clauses, each dependent clause has its own line.

Example 3.8(a)
Sentence with too many dependent clauses

Draft: The officer pulled over a woman
             who was driving a green car
             when she ran a red light
             while she was talking to a friend on her cell phone
             after she had had a fight with her boyfriend
             even though she had already broken up with him
             and gave her a ticket.

In Example 3.8(a), the main idea of the sentence is *the officer pulled over a woman and gave her a ticket.* Everything else nested inside is a dependent clause. Obviously those nested dependent clauses are causing some problems.

Dependent clauses look a lot like independent clauses, with one major exception. Dependent clauses begin with a word or two that make them *depend* on the rest of the sentence for meaning. Take a close look at Example 3.8(a). You'll see that each line could be its own sentence, but only if you deleted the bold word at the beginning. Those bold words are SUBORDINATING CONJUNCTIONS and RELATIVE PRONOUNS. These little words singlehandedly turn an independent clause into a dependent clause.

Because these little words turn independent clauses into dependent clauses, the easiest way for you to spot a dependent clause is to look for either a subordinating conjunction or a relative pronoun. At least that is the easiest way once you know what subordinating conjunctions and relative pronouns are.

Understanding how subordinating conjunctions work might be a little easier once you see a few more subordinating conjunctions. Chart 3.8(1) has a list of the most common subordinating conjunctions.

Grammar Reminder

Remember that a **conjunction** is a word used to join other words, phrases, or clauses and that different kinds of conjunctions express different relationships between the words, phrases, or clauses that they join.

Subordinating conjunctions introduce a clause but demonstrate how it is lesser than — subordinate to — the rest of the sentence.

Chart 3.8(1)
Most Common Subordinating Conjunctions

after	although	as
as if	because	before
even though	how	if
in order that	once	rather than
since	so that	than
that	though	unless
until	when	where
whether	while	why

Seeing this list might give you a better sense of what a subordinating conjunction is. And, once you get the idea of what a subordinating conjunction is and how it works, you will realize that you probably do not need to commit the list to memory. Instead, you can use your computer's find function to search for some of the more common subordinating conjunctions. When you see one, you can almost be sure that a dependent clause is lurking right behind.

Because relative pronouns work in much the same way as subordinating conjunctions, it might be helpful to have a list of those as well. That list is in Chart 3.8(2).

Chart 3.8(2)
Relative Pronouns

that	which	who
whom	whose	when
where	why	

Whenever you see a dependent clause — especially if you see multiple dependent clauses in one sentence or dependent clauses in several consecutive sentences — you should consider revising the sentence. The revision process for a sentence with too many dependent clauses is a bit more complicated than it is for a sentence with too many independent clauses.

To make the revision process more manageable, start by deciding whether the dependent clause is necessary to the meaning of the sentence. If it is, then the dependent clause is a RESTRICTIVE MODIFIER and should probably just stay put. Take, for instance, the sentence in Example 3.8(b). A relative pronoun — *who* — introduces a dependent clause — *who had a warrant out for her arrest*. But the dependent clause is necessary to the meaning of the sentence. If Officer Dennis had arrested some other citizen — one who did not have a warrant out for her arrest — then Officer Dennis would likely be in big trouble.

Example 3.8(b)
Sentence with a restrictive modifier

Draft: Officer Dennis arrested the citizen **who had a warrant out for her arrest.**

If the dependent clause provides information that is helpful, but not necessary, to the meaning of the sentence, it is a NONRESTRICTIVE MODIFIER and you have a few options. First, you could pull it out of the sentence — and your document — altogether. If you include too much unimportant information, your reader will struggle to identify the important information in your sentence. Your job is to identify what is important about the sen-

---

Grammar Reminder

A **pronoun** is a word that you can use in place of a noun. For example, the personal pronoun *she* can replace the noun *woman*.

There are several different kinds of pronouns. A **relative pronoun** is a pronoun that introduces a dependent clause. Like all pronouns, relative pronouns allow you to link together two thoughts without repeating the noun.

For example, to link together the ideas *the officer pulled over a woman* and *the woman was driving a green car*, you simply replace the second *the woman* with a relative pronoun and put the two ideas into a single sentence. The result: *the officer pulled over a woman who was driving a green car.*

Grammar Reminder

A **restrictive modifier** is a modifier that further defines the word that it is modifying and therefore contains information that is essential to the sentence.

A **nonrestrictive modifier** is a modifier that simply gives additional information about a word that has already been clearly defined. It's helpful, but not necessary, in the sentence.

For more on restrictive and nonrestrictive modifiers and how they are punctuated, take a look at Editing Strategy 5.6-5.

tence and then edit out any information that is not essential to your meaning. You will see that in Example 3.8(c), the writer decided that the dependent clause *where they had camped, hunted, and fished for years* was a nonrestrictive modifier that could come out of the sentence altogether.

Example 3.8(c)
Sentence with a nonrestrictive modifier revised by eliminating the information in the nonrestrictive modifier

Draft: The Jordan family's possession of the Horseshoe Lake Woods, **where they had camped, hunted, and fished for years,** was open and notorious.

Revision: The Jordan family's possession of the Horseshoe Lake Woods was open and notorious.

If you don't want to completely remove the tangentially related information, consider including it in a separate sentence. In Example 3.8(d), the dependent clause *who had a sign on the edge of the property* is an important idea, but not crucial to the sentence. It should get—it even deserves—its own sentence.

Example 3.8(d)
Sentence with a nonrestrictive modifier revised by putting information in the nonrestrictive modifier into a new sentence

Draft: The claimant, **who had a sign on the edge of the property indicating his ownership,** maintained a sealing bench, house, smokehouse, well, and tent for storing boat parts on the beach-front, semi-wilderness property. *Peters v. Juneau-Douglas Girl Scout Council,* 519 P.2d 826, 828 (Alaska 1974).

Revision: The claimant maintained a sealing bench, house, smokehouse, well, and tent for storing boat parts on the beach-front, semi-wilderness property. *Peters v. Juneau-Douglas Girl Scout Council,* 519 P.2d 826, 828 (Alaska 1974). The claimant had a sign on the edge of the property indicating his ownership, but the sign fell off its post. *Id*

What Is a Modifier Anyway?

Why is a dependent clause also called a modifier? And how can a prepositional phrase also be a modifier? Why are there so many different grammatical terms for the very same thing?

The answer is quite simple. Modifier is the generic term for any word, phrase, or clause that modifies or qualifies something.

Modifiers are usually either (1) adjectives used to modify or describe a noun or pronoun or (2) adverbs that are used to modify or qualify a verb, an adjective, or another adverb.

Try not to get hung up on the grammatical jargon. *Modifier* and *qualifier* are actually just words that describe the job that certain words, phrases, and clauses are doing.

✍ Editing Strategy 3.9
Check for Too Many Prepositional Phrases in a Single Sentence

After checking your draft for strings of independent clauses and nests of dependent clauses, do a quick check for sentences with too many PREPOSITIONS. A preposition, like a subordinating conjunction, is a signal that you have included a modifier in the sentence. And, while a single prepositional phrase in a sentence is not necessarily a problem, multiple prepositional phrases will affect the vigor of your writing.

> **Grammar Reminder**
>
> A **preposition** is simply a word (see Chart 3.9) that you group with a noun to form a prepositional phrase.

So, check your draft for prepositions and pay close attention to any sentence that has multiple prepositional phrases. Chart 3.9 has a list of some common prepositions. Just like the list of subordinating clauses, this list might be useful at first but become increasingly unnecessary as you really start to understand why prepositional phrases cause problems.

Chart 3.9
Some Common Prepositions

above	across	against
along	around	before
behind	below	beside
between	by	during
inside	like	near
of	onto	over
	since	

Consider editing any sentence that has multiple prepositional phrases. You may discover that some prepositional phrases do not need to be prepositional phrases at all—they can take a different form. The revised sentence in Example 3.9(a) demonstrates this approach. The writer edited out two of the prepositional phrases by rewriting the sentence in active voice. (See Editing Strategy 3.4 for the fix.) She also decided that expanding the prepositional phrase *across the lake* into the dependent clause *which was located across the lake* would result in fewer prepositional phrases and thus a more clear sentence. Finally, the prepositional phrase *during the year* became the much shorter (and not prepositional) phrase *year round*. These fixes led the reader to discover that the sentence was a little long, so she revised again.

Example 3.9(a)
Sentence with too many prepositional phrases revised by changing prepositional phrases' forms

Draft:	The property **across** the lake was cared **for by** the Jordan family **during** the year and hiked on **by** the neighbors **between** May and August.
Revision:	The Jordan family cared **for** the property, which was located across the lake, year round, and the family's neighbors hiked **on** the property **between** May and August.
Second Revision:	The Jordan family cared **for** the property, which was located across the lake, year round. The family's neighbors hiked **on** the property **between** May and August.

Or you might discover that some prepositional phrases contain information that is not really necessary to the meaning of the sentence at all and can be deleted. In Example 3.9(b), the writer realized that the prepositional phrase *across the lake* was actually not necessary.

Example 3.9(b)
Sentence with too many prepositional phrases revised by omitting information in the prepositional phrase

Draft:	The property **across** the lake was cared **for by** the Jordan family **during** the year and hiked on **by** the neighbors **between** May and August.
Revision:	The Jordan family cared **for** the property year round. The family's neighbors hiked **on** the property **between** May and August.

3. Omit Surplus Words

The final step in ensuring that your sentences are de-cluttered and vigorous is to get rid of unnecessary words. By getting rid of unnecessary dependent clauses and prepositional phrases, you have already gone a long way to culling the clutter from your sentences. The final step is just getting rid of those last bits of clutter that are going to distract your reader and take the vigor from your writing.

✍ Editing Strategy 3.10
Check for Wordy Phrases

In a sweep for that last bit of clutter, you are checking your writing for wordy phrases that can bloat even a short sentence. Certain phrases almost guarantee wordiness. But there is no way to write an exhaustive list of wordy phrases. Instead, you should develop your own list. Check for the most common wordy phrases, listed in Chart 3.10, but then comb carefully through your writing to find places where you have used three words when one word will do the job.

Chart 3.10
Common Wordy Phrases and Replacements

Wordy Phrase	Replacement
despite the fact that	although, even though, despite
due to the fact	because, since
whether or not	whether
came to an agreement	agreed
except when	unless
in some instances	sometimes
on the basis of	based on, because of
in the event that	if
in an angry (etc.) manner	angrily, etc.
not only … but also	and, both
in regard to	about
by means of	by
in view of the fact that	because, since, for
subsequent to	after

When you find a wordy phrase, just replace it with a less wordy alternative. Deciding on the less wordy alternative will depend, to a large extent, on the meaning of the phrase in the sentence that you are using. Example 3.10(a) demonstrates how easy—and effective—this change can be.

Example 3.10(a)
Sentences with wordy phrase revised by replacing wordy phrases

Draft: **Despite the fact that** the building that the defendant entered was not a dwelling, he was still charged with first-degree burglary.

Revision: **Although** the building that the defendant entered was not a dwelling, he was still charged with first-degree burglary.

Draft: The issue is **whether or not** the building is regularly occupied.

Revision: The issue is **whether** the building is regularly occupied.

Draft: The police officer questioned the suspect **in an angry manner.**

Revision: The police officer questioned the suspect **angrily.**

While you should thoroughly check your writing for wordiness, you may find that you have already purged some of the wordiness from your writing by using concrete subjects and strong, active verbs. For instance, by replacing *it is* with a concrete subject and an active verb, you will be forcing yourself to fix wordy phrases like *it is important to note* or *it is obvious that*.

4. Combining Vigor and Variety

Writing short sentences, using active voice, and omitting surplus words are tools for creating vigorous writing. But writing *only* short sentences, using *only* active voice, and omitting *all* surplus words probably would not result in vigorous writing. You must still leave room for variety. You should vary your sentence length and you might occasionally use a wordy construction. The key, however, is to be thoughtful about the variety that you include in your writing. Make sure that it is adding to the picture that you are painting rather than bogging your reader down.

Vigorous Writing:
The Exercises

In all of these exercises, focus on the editing strategies that are specifically assigned. Also, feel free to make notes about places where you might choose not to employ an editing strategy or places where an editing strategy that wasn't specifically assigned might be helpful.

1. Use Concrete Subjects and Strong, Active Verbs

Use Editing Strategies 3.1 through 3.5 to edit the following passage from the memo on burglary. As you edit, notice instances of passive voice or nominalizations that you would retain and make a note about why.

In *Nollen*, it was held that a semi-truck trailer was a building because it had been adapted for use as a business. *Id.* at 789. A semi-truck trailer was used by St. Vincent de Paul as a donation center. *Id.* at 788. A truck would tow a trailer to the transfer station, but then the driver would detach the trailer and leave it for a period of time. *Id.* In addition to the driver leaving the trailer for a period of time, St. Vincent placed a temporary stairway next to the trailer so that members of the public could walk up the stairs and into the trailer to make their donations. *Id.* There were also permanent signs near the trailer advertising it as a donation collection station. *Id.* The nature of the court's decision related to the adaptation of the trailer from its ordinary use as a vehicle to use in the business of collecting and redistributing donations. *Id.* at 789. The requirements of the statute are not that the adaptation of a vehicle be permanent, so the changes to the trailer were sufficient even though the trailer was not permanently located at the transfer station. *Id.* Thus, it was held that the trailer was a building. *Id.*

On the other hand, in *State v. Scott*, 590 P.2d 743, 744 (Or. App. 1979), it was held that a railroad boxcar was not a building because it had not been modified to be used as anything other than a vehicle. In *Scott*, a railroad boxcar was entered by the defendant with the intent to commit a crime. *See id.* However, because the railroad boxcar was not a building, the court dealt with the defendant's burglary conviction by overturning it. *Id.* The court noted that there could conceivably be an adaptation of the boxcar for business. *Id.* However, because the boxcar in that case had not been changed in any way from its ordinary purpose — that is, because it was still simply a "structure on wheels designed for the storage of goods and their transportation" — the court held that it was not a building. *Id.*

2. Write Uncluttered Sentences

Use Editing Strategies 3.6 through 3.9 to edit the following passage from the memo on burglary.

Here, the mobile bakery that Mr. Dennison entered is a building because it has been adapted for carrying on business and the mobile bakery, which was originally simply a utility van, has been changed and modified, much in the same way that the trailer in *Nollen* was modified and stands in contrast to the boxcar in *Scott*. Like the trailer in *Nollen*, which was detached from the truck that towed it, the van's awning was open and extending from the side of the van and chairs were positioned under that awning and therefore these changes make both the trailer in *Nollen* and the mobile bakery unsuitable for use as a vehicle while they are in business. But Ms. Carlson has made even more changes to the van, including putting down laminate flooring inside the van, adding refrigerator space for her products along the interior wall of the van, and adding a sink and small bathroom beside the refrigerator space, which make it markedly different from the boxcar in *Scott*, where there was no evidence that the boxcar had been modified at all. All of these changes demonstrate that the van has been adapted for a new purpose.

3. Omit Surplus Words

Use Editing Strategy 3.10 to edit the following passage from the memo on burglary.

The mobile bakery that Justin Dennison broke into is a building under Oregon burglary law. The State can establish that a structure is a building in one of two ways: (1) by proving that the structure is a "building" in the "ordinary meaning" of that term or (2) by proving that it is a "booth, vehicle, boat, aircraft, or other structure adapted for overnight accommodation of persons or for carrying on business therein." Or. Rev. Stat. 164.205(1) (2013). In view of the fact that the van is not a building within the ordinary meaning of that term, the question is whether or not it is a vehicle adapted for overnight accommodation of persons or for carrying on business therein.

Despite the fact that the van is occasionally used as a place of overnight accommodation, it has not been sufficiently adapted for overnight accommodation under the statute. However, it has been adapted for carrying on business. A vehicle is adapted if it is changed or modified so that it is suitable for a new or different use. *State v. Nollen*, 100 P.3d 788, 789 (Or. App. 2004). This new or different use must be a business use, which is simply "'a commercial or industrial enterprise.'" *Id.* (*quoting* Webster's Third New Int'l Dictionary 23 (unabridged ed. 1993)).

Chapter 4

Clear Writing

"One should aim not at being possible to understand, but at being impossible to misunderstand." — *Quintillian*

After you've edited for organization and vigor, the next step is to edit for clarity. Clear writing is writing that is easily and immediately understandable. Clear writing won't throw up barriers or lay down speed bumps. It won't send your reader running for a dictionary or puzzling over your meaning. So, when you're editing for clarity, you're really just looking for those barriers and speed bumps.

Careless word choice can be a significant barrier to clear writing. To avoid careless word choice, be on the lookout for unclear, inaccurate, or inconsistent language. Also be sure that you're looking for grammatical problems like ambiguous pronouns and subjects and verbs that don't agree. Next, put those carefully chosen words in the right place. Make sure that modifiers are close to what they modify and subjects are close to their verbs. By pulling down the barriers and getting rid of the speed bumps — by editing for clarity — you'll be making sure that your reader's path is clear. Your writing will be better and her reading will be easier. Everybody will win.

Clear Writing:
The Editing Checklist

1. Choose Words Carefully

✍ 4.1 Check That Language Is Clear

Look for legal jargon and terms of art in your writing. Replace all of the legal jargon. Keep the terms of art only if you are writing to a law-trained reader.

✍ 4.2 Check That Language Is Accurate

Keep a list of the words that you most often confuse or misuse (is it *find* or *hold*? *affect* or *effect*?) and then use your computer's find function to look for them. Edit to make sure the word you've chosen is really the word you mean to use.

✍ 4.3 Check That Language Is Consistent

Look for elegant variation that diminishes clarity and replace the variation with consistent language.

✍ 4.4 Check for Ambiguous Pronouns

Search your writing for pronouns. Check each pronoun to make sure that it refers clearly to the right noun. If the pronoun could actually be referring to two (or more) possible nouns, then the pronoun is ambiguous. Fix the ambiguity by turning the pronoun back into a noun.

✍ 4.5 Check for Remote Pronouns

After eliminating ambiguous pronouns, make sure that any remaining pronouns aren't too far away from the nouns to which they refer.

✍ 4.6 Check That Pronouns and Their Antecedents Agree

As you finish up with pronouns, make sure that you've replaced singular nouns with singular pronouns and plural nouns with plural pronouns.

✍ 4.7 Check That Subjects and Verbs Agree

In every sentence, make sure that the subject and verb agree. In other words, singular nouns need singular verbs and plural nouns need plural verbs.

2. Place Words Carefully

✍ 4.8 Check That Subjects and Verbs Are Close Together

Find both the subject and the verb in your sentence. If more than seven or eight words separate the subject and verb, find a way to get them closer together.

✍ 4.9 Check for Misplaced Modifiers

Search your writing for modifiers. Where you see a modifier, make sure that it's in the right place. Typically, this means that the modifier should be close to the word that it modifies.

✍ 4.10 Check for Dangling Modifiers

Take another look at all the modifiers you've identified. Make sure that each modifier actually modifies a word or phrase in the sentence. If it doesn't—if it only hints at what it's supposed to modify—it's a dangling modifier that needs to be replaced.

✍ 4.11 Check for Squinting Modifiers

Take one last look at those modifiers. If you see a modifier that is sitting between two words or phrases and it could conceivably modify either of those words or phrases, it's a squinting modifier. Revise the sentence so that the modifier is clearly referring to what it is meant to modify.

Clear Writing:
The Details

1. Choose Words Carefully

You've probably heard someone say—at least once—that words are a lawyer's tools of trade. Well, for better or worse, it's true. Words are what we have to work with. So we'd better be good at using them. Just as a carpenter chooses her tools carefully (she doesn't use a hammer when she should be using a screwdriver), a writer has to choose her tools carefully (she shouldn't say *must* when she means *should*).

But choosing the right word can be a little more complicated than choosing between a hammer and a screwdriver. Often, there are many different words that will do the job. When choosing the best tool, then, you should think about choosing the word that is not only clear but also accurate. (The word *affect* is pretty clear, but if you mean to use the word *effect*, then your word choice is not at all accurate.) When you've chosen the clearest, most accurate word, you'll know that you've chosen the right tool. Then, take a minute to make sure that you're using the tool the right way—that your word choice is consistent and grammatically correct. Using the tool the right way is just as important as picking the right tool in the first place. And this is really solid advice from someone who has on more than one occasion tried to use a hammer on a screw.

> ✍ Editing Strategy 4.1
> **Check That Language Is Clear**

When you write as a lawyer, you will always have a very clear goal. You will be explaining your prediction for a particular client, or persuading a court, or advising a client. But no matter what your particular goal, your writing must be clear. In order to have any success explaining, persuading, or advising, you must be clear.

To know whether your word choice is clear, you need to know something about your reader and be able to recognize the difference between plain language, legal jargon, and terms of art.

First, you need to know who your reader is. While this is always true, it might be most important when you are thinking about word choice. The words you choose when writing to a client might be different from the words you choose when writing to another lawyer or a judge.

Once you know who your reader is, you can choose your language carefully. Here are the rules: (1) you can use plain language when you're writing to any reader, (2) you can use terms of art when you are writing to a law-trained reader, (3) you can use legal jargon only when you are talking to yourself and you are absolutely sure no one else is listening.

These rules, of course, require you to know the difference between plain language, terms of art, and legal jargon. Plain language is, well, language that is plain. If you would say a word in a conversation with a friend (law school classmates and lawyers don't count here), then it's probably plain language. If on the other hand, you find a word in your writing that you wouldn't use in a conversation with a friend, then it's probably either a term of art or legal jargon. Because you wouldn't say *hereinafter* in a conversation with a friend, it's not plain language.

The difference between a term of art and legal jargon is that legal jargon can be easily replaced with a plain language alternative while terms of art cannot. The operative words here are *easily replaced*. Take a look, for example, at Example 4.1(a). You'll see that the word *arguendo* was easily replaced by the phrase *for the sake of argument*. So, *arguendo* is replaceable jargon. (Better yet, it might just be jargon that can be taken out altogether and not replaced at all. Take a closer look at the second revision in Example 4.1(a).)

Example 4.1(a)
Sentence with replaceable jargon revised by replacing jargon

Draft: Even assuming **arguendo** that the defendant was seized by the police, the evidence should still be admissible because its discovery was sufficiently attenuated from the illegal seizure.

Revision: Even assuming **for the sake of argument** that the defendant was seized by the police, the evidence should still be admissible because its discovery was sufficiently attenuated from the illegal seizure.

Revision: Even assuming that the defendant was seized by the police, the evidence should still be admissible because its discovery was sufficiently attenuated from the illegal seizure.

If a word can't be easily replaced—if it would require you to include extensive explanation—then it's a term of art. Basic terms of art include *consideration*, *negligence*, and *jurisdiction*. But, remember, you can use terms of art only with other lawyers who will understand the meaning of the terms. So, while you might write about *consideration* in a memo to another associate, you would never use that term—without some explanation—in a letter to a client. With clients, or any non-lawyer, you're going to have to give the full explanation in plain language.

Chart 4.1(1) lists some legal jargon and replacements for the jargon. Chart 4.1(2) lists some terms of art that simply don't have easy replacements. (In other words, you get to use them with other lawyers.) But these lists are not exhaustive. So, search for these words in your own writing, but then be careful in your writing to also search for any words that have a plain language alternative. Replace them.

Chart 4.1(1)
Legal Jargon and Replacements

arguendo = for the sake of argument
pursuant to = under or according to
thenceforth = from that time on, after that
cease = stop
commence = begin, start
during such time as = while
effectuate = carry out, try
forthwith = immediately
prior to = before
render = make
procure = obtain, get
until such time as = until
in order to = to
indicate = show
incumbent upon = must

Chart 4.1(2)
Terms of Art

consideration	negligence	jursidiction
certiorari	de novo	ex parte
respondeat superior	prima facie	mens rea
stare decisis	res ipsa loquitor	

Pompous Language

Legal jargon has a closely related cousin. Professors Anne Enquist and Laurel Currie Oates, in their book *Just Writing: Grammar, Punctuation, and Style for the Legal Writer*, call it pompous language.

Pompous language is the language that we sometimes use to, well, let's be honest, make us sound smart. We "secure a position at a fine institution" rather than "take a job at a very good firm." We "ascertain" that we "utilize" and "finalize" rather than just "making sure" that we "use" or "finish."

The problem, of course, is that no amount of pompous language is going to make an unclear or unformed idea sound smart. Sure, it might provide a little bit of a disguise, but it's not going to fool your reader. And if you're not trying to fool your reader — if your ideas are clear and well thought out — the disguise isn't necessary at all. Your reader will appreciate the clarity of your thought and the effort it took to make that thought so easily accessible.

✐ Editing Strategy 4.2
Check That Language Is Accurate

Even if you choose a word that is simple and clear, you still need to be sure that it's the right word. The right word is not only the word that means what you think it means (with a nod here, of course, to Inigo Montoya) but also the word that has the right connotation.

First, choose the word that really means what you think it means. Now, most of the time this is easy. Once in a while, you will need to look up a word in a dictionary because you think you know what it means but anyone who doesn't live in your head — or who didn't grow up with your family or have a certain teacher — might assign it a different meaning. And there are definitely some words that always seem, for one reason or another, to be a bit tricky. Following is a list of some of those words. Check for these words in your writing, but add to this list as you find other words or pairs of words that just seem to trip you up.

(1) **Find/Hold.** The difference between *find* and *hold* is an important one for lawyers. Judges *find* facts. So, typically, you'll use the word *find* when you're talking about lower courts rather than appellate courts, as in Example 4.2(a).

Example 4.2(a)
***Find* used accurately**

Revision: The trial judge **found** that the plaintiff used the
                 property for hiking and camping during the summer.

A court's *holding*, on the other hand, is the answer to the issue. The revision in Example 4.2(b) used *held* right.

Example 4.2(b)
***Hold* used accurately**

Revision: The court **held** that the plaintiff's use of the property
                 was open and notorious.

Sometimes, though, the court is making neither a *finding* nor a *holding*. If a court is stating a principle that is part of the analysis but that doesn't directly answer the issue, then it's most clear—and most accurate—to say that the court *concluded* or *determined* or *stated*. Take a look at Example 4.2(c) to see how *find*, *hold*, and *concluded* can work together.

Example 4.2(c)
***Find / conclude / hold* used accurately**

Revision: The trial court **found** that the plaintiff used the property for hiking and camping during the summer. The appellate court accepted this finding and **concluded** that this use was enough to put a reasonably diligent landowner on notice that the plaintiff was laying claim to the land. *Nome 2000*, 799 P.2d at 310. Thus, the court **held** that the plaintiff's use of the property was open and notorious. *Id.*

But be careful when choosing a verb that's not *find* or *held*. Because, while a court can *conclude* or *determine*, courts don't *feel* or *argue*.

(2) **Affect / Effect.** Probably the easiest (but not perfect) way to remember the difference between *affect* and *effect* is that *affect* is typically used as a verb—it's an action—while *effect* is typically used as a noun—it's a thing.

Affect, when used as a verb, means "to have an influence on somebody or something." Take a look at Example 4.2(d) where *affected* means *influenced*.

Example 4.2(d)
Affect used as a verb

Revision: The defendant's pleas **affected** (or influenced) the judge.

Effect, when used as a noun, most often means "a result." In Example 4.2(e), *effect* really means *result*.

Example 4.2(e)
Effect used as a noun

Revision: The **effect** (or result—picture the judge in tears here) was surprising.

Keep in mind, though, that both *affect* and *effect* can switch roles. When *affect* is used as a noun it means, roughly, "an emotional response."

Example 4.2(f)
Affect used a noun

Revision: The judge was surprised by the defendant's relatively happy **affect** (or emotional response—picture the defendant responding happily despite the circumstances).

When *effect* is used as a verb it means "to bring about."

Example 4.2(g)
Effect used as a verb

Revision: The trial judge ultimately decided that the best way to **effect** (or bring about) change in the defendant's life was to sentence her to probation.

To deal with this tricky pair, try substituting a synonym or even the definition of the word for the word itself. Take a look at Examples 4.2(d) through 4.2(g). Notice how the definition of the word (in parentheses behind the word itself) could actually substitute for the word in the sentence. So if the synonym (or definition) works in the sentence, you've chosen the right word.

(3) **Number/Amount.** To tackle this particular pair, you need to know the difference between a COUNT NOUN and a NONCOUNT NOUN. Because these particular grammar words are so descriptive, they're very easy to remember. Count nouns refer to things that can be counted—people, or cars, or fruit. Noncount nouns refer to things or abstractions that can't be counted—air, or salt, or patience.

Keeping that distinction in mind, here's the rule: when you are writing about count nouns—people, cars, fruit—you use *number*. When you are writing about noncount nouns—air, salt, patience—you use *amount*. Example 4.2(h) follows this rule.

> **Grammar Reminder**
>
> **Count nouns** refer to persons, places, and things that can be counted, like bottles.
>
> **Noncount nouns**—sometimes called **mass nouns**—refer to things or abstractions that can't be counted, like champagne.
>
> One way to spot the difference between a count noun and a non-count noun is that you can't make a nouncount noun plural. So no matter how much champagne you have, you'll never have *champagnes*. But you will have many *bottles* of champagne.

Example 4.2(h)
Sentence with *number* and *amount* used accurately

Revision: A **number of people** were dissatisfied with the judge's final decision. But the judge showed a tremendous **amount of patience** as he addressed the crowded courtroom.

---

(4) **Fewer/Less.** Once again, the difference between count and nouncount nouns is going to be helpful when you are choosing between *fewer* and *less*. When you are writing about count nouns—objections, mo-

tions, trials—you use *fewer*. On the other hand, when you are writing about noncount nouns—work, trustworthiness—you use *less*. The draft sentence in Example 4.2(i) gets the rule only half right. The revised sentence fixes the problem, using *fewer* with the count noun.

Example 4.2(i)
Sentence with *less* used incorrectly, revised by substituting *fewer* for *less*

Draft: The lawyer decided that making **less** objections was the key to winning over the jury. However, the jury ultimately decided that the plaintiff was a **less** reliable witness than the defendant.

Revision: The lawyer decided that making **fewer** objections was the key to winning over the jury. However, the jury ultimately decided that the plaintiff was a **less** reliable witness than the defendant.

---

(5) **Many/Much.** Here we go again. To get this one right, pair *many* with count nouns. Pair *much* with noncount nouns. Example 4.2(j) demonstrates.

Example 4.2(j)
Sentence with *many* and *much* used accurately

Revision: The lawyer made so **many** motions that the judge nearly lost count. And yet, when the trial was over, the lawyer still had so **much** work left that she returned to her office for several hours.

---

(6) **As/Like.** To navigate these two words, which often seem to mean the same thing, just remember that they have different functions. *As* is a subordinating conjunction. *Like* is a preposition.

As is a subordinating conjunction, which means that it introduces a clause and sets up the relationship between what comes before and after it (take a look back at Chart 3.8(1) for more detail). In Example 4.2(k), you'll see that *as* introduces the clause (remember, a clause is a string of words that looks just like a sentence—it has both a subject and a verb) that follows it; it's a subordinating conjunction.

Example 4.2(k)
Sentence with *as* used accurately

Revision: The judge ruled on this motion **as** he ruled on the last motion.

Not only does *as* introduce the clause that comes after it in Example 4.2(k) but it also sets up the relationship between what comes before and after. While *he ruled on the last motion* could be its own sentence, it's not (which is pretty much the definition of a clause, remember?). Instead, it relies on the first half of the sentence for its meaning, and the subordinating conjunction helps supply that meaning.

Like, on the other hand, isn't a conjunction. It's a preposition. (Take a look back at Chart 3.9(1).) So, you aren't supposed to use it to introduce a whole clause. It only gets to introduce a noun phrase. (Remember a phrase is just a group of words hanging out together without looking or acting like a sentence.) Take a look at Example 4.2(l), which says essentially the same thing as Example 4.2(k) but in a different way.

Example 4.2(l)
Sentence with *like* used accurately

Revision: The judge's ruling on this motion was **like** his ruling on
                  the last motion.

Notice that Example 4.2(l) conveys the same meaning as Example 4.2(k), but notice the way in which it is different. In Example 4.2(l), the writer uses the word *like* to introduce the noun phrase *his ruling on the last motion*.

If you would have used the word *like* in the sentences in both Example 4.2(k) and 4.2(l), you aren't alone. *Like* is frequently used as a conjunction—especially in conversation. Just try not to let this common, informal usage creep into your formal writing.

(7) **Because/Since/As.** The word *as* is such a troublemaker that it makes this list twice. Not only can it cause trouble when a writer is making comparisons (*as/like*), but it can also cause trouble when a writer is trying to demonstrate a causal relationship (*because/since/as*).

There are lots of different ways to demonstrate a causal relationship in writing. But, really, that's just a fancy way of saying that there are lots of different ways to say *because*. There are wordy ways to say *because* (for example, *due to the fact that*), but you already know to avoid those. There are also seemingly fancy ways to say *because*. *Since* and *as* fall into this category. To some writers, they just sound better. The problem is that they're often less clear.

Clarity is particularly a problem for the word *as*. *As* can be used to mean *because*. But it more typically means *while*. And this difference can cause problems. Take a look at the draft Example 4.2(m), and see if it doesn't give you at least a little trouble.

Example 4.2(m)
Sentence with *as* used to demonstrate causal relationship, revised by replacing *as* with *because*

Draft: The court sustained the objection, **as** the testimony was clearly hearsay.

Revision: The court sustained the objection **because** the testimony was clearly hearsay.

Notice how, when you read the draft in Example 4.2(m), you have to pause, even if just for a fraction of a second, to adjust your expectations for the second part of the sentence. (When you first started reading it, you might have pictured the court overruling the objection *while* the testimony was going on.) In the revision, the writer's meaning is immediately clear.

The easy fix here is to simply avoid using *as* when you really mean *because*. The word *since* can be a better substitute for *because*, but you have to be careful with it as well. Take a look at the draft sentence in Example 4.2(n).

Example 4.2(n)
Sentence with *since* used to demonstrate causal relationship, revised by replacing *since* with *because*

Draft: He had been available for a meeting **since** the second matter had settled.

Revision: He had been available for a meeting **because** the second matter had settled.

The draft sentence in Example 4.2(n) seems perfectly clear until you realize that it could actually mean two different things. It could mean that he had been available for a meeting *since* the second matter settled a week ago. Or it could mean that he had been available for this morning's meeting *because* the second matter settled.

Since often refers to how much time has passed, so using it rather than *because* may cause your reader to stumble a bit. The bottom line: when you mean *because*, *because* is probably the clearest word to use.

(8) **If/Whether.** *If* and *whether* are both words that lawyers use a lot. So it makes sense to know the difference between the two. You use *if* when you are expressing a condition. And you use *whether* when you are showing that there are two possible alternatives. The next two examples come from client letters and demonstrate the difference between *if* and *whether*.

In Example 4.2(o), the writer has used *if* to express a condition.

> **Example 4.2(o)**
> ***If* used correctly**
>
> Revision: You do not need to be at the hearing, but please contact me **if** you plan to attend.

In Example 4.2(o), the writer is telling the client that the client needs to call the attorney only on the condition that she plans to attend the hearing. So, if the client doesn't plan to attend, there's no need to contact the attorney.

In Example 4.2(p), the writer has used *whether* to show that there are two options.

> **Example 4.2(p)**
> ***Whether* used correctly**
>
> Revision: You do not need to be at the hearing, but it would be helpful for me to know in advance **whether** you will be there.

In Example 4.2(p), the attorney wants to hear from the client one way or the other. The attorney will be expecting the client to call with a yes or a no.

(9) **Assure/Insure/Ensure.** Here's the easiest way to remember the difference between these three similar-sounding words: you *assure* people, you *insure* money, and you *ensure* that things happen.

Assure means to make promises to or convince. You can only do this with people. Take a look at Example 4.2(q).

> **Example 4.2(q)**
> ***Assure* used correctly**
>
> Revision: The lawyer **assured** her client that they were close to a settlement.

Insure means to arrange for compensation in case of damage or loss. This one is easy to remember because it's what *insur*ance companies do. In Example 4.2(r), the client probably turned to the insurance company for that insurance.

> **Example 4.2(r)**
> ***Insure* used correctly**
>
> Revision: The client was careful to use a part of the settlement to **insure** against future loss.

Ensure means to make certain that some thing occurs or some event takes place. Obviously, you need a thing or an event in the sentence for this one. Take a look at Example 4.2(s).

Example 4.2(s)
***Ensure* used correctly**

Revision: To **ensure** that she was able to reach a settlement on behalf of her client, the lawyer spent a great deal of time researching the law.

---

(10) **Beside/Besides**. The difference between *beside* and *besides*, in a very literal way, is just a single letter. But these two words are much farther apart than their spelling might suggest. In fact, they mean entirely different things.

Beside means at the side of. Take a look at Example 4.2(t).

Example 4.2(t)
***Beside* used correctly**

Revision: There was no one **beside** the defendant at the table.

The sentence in Example 4.2(t) describes a scenario in which the defendant has an empty chair next to him, but there still may have been others at the table.

Besides means except or in addition to. Take a look at Example 4.2(u).

Example 4.2(u)
***Besides* used correctly**

Revision: There was no one **besides** the defendant at the table.

The sentence in Example 4.2(u) describes a scenario in which not only does the defendant have empty chairs beside him, but he is the only one at the table.

Using *beside* when you really mean *besides* may work sometimes. But there are times (take the sentences in Example 4.2(t) and 4.2(u)) where substituting *beside* for *besides* will result in ambiguity. And ambiguous writing is the opposite of clear writing.

(11) **Imply/Infer**. These two verbs are often mistaken for one another. Here's the difference: you *imply* if you are the speaker or writer, but you *infer* if you are the listener or reader.

Imply means to hint at or suggest.

Example 4.2(v)
Imply **used correctly**

Revision: In her demand letter, the employee **implied** that she was
            ready to file a lawsuit.

Infer means to deduce or conclude.

Example 4.2(w)
Infer **used correctly**

Revision: However, given that the employee gave the employer
            three months to reply to the letter, the employer
            inferred that the employee was not in fact ready to file a
            lawsuit.

---

(12) **Then/Than**. Even if you know the difference between these two
words, you might still find that as you write, you choose the wrong
one.

Remember, *than* is used only in comparisons. Example 4.2(x) uses
than in a comparison.

Example 4.2(x)
Than **used correctly**

Revision: Here, the defendant's argument is even stronger **than** it
            was in *Olson*.

Then, on the other hand, can be used to mean quite a few different
things (*at that point in time, next, if, in that case*). Example 4.2(y) uses
then to mean *in that case*.

Example 4.2(y)
Then **used correctly**

Revision: If the defendant hopes to make that argument on
            appeal, **then** she must preserve the error.

The easiest way to deal with this pair is simply to make sure that it's
on your editing checklist. When you edit for clarity, make sure that
you've used *than* only for comparisons and *then* everywhere else.

(13) **Principle/Principal**. Okay, now for the homophones. These pairs
are tricky because they sound exactly the same in spoken English, which
makes it even more difficult to remember which is which.

A *principle* is a truth, law, or doctrine. It's almost always a noun. Take a look at Example 4.2(z).

Example 4.2(z)
***Principle* used correctly**

Revision: The doctrine of adverse possession is based, in part, on the **principle** that the true owner should be put on notice of someone else's claim to the property.

A *principal*, on the other hand, is almost always an adjective. It means chief, primary, or most important. In Example 4.2(aa), *principal* means primary.

Example 4.2(aa)
***Principal* used correctly**

Revision: The **principal** reason that the judge rejected the adverse possession claim was that the true owner of the property did not have sufficient notice of someone else's claim to the property.

But—and here's where it gets a little tricky—*principal* can also be used as a noun. In fact, lawyers tend to do this quite a bit. In agency law, lawyers talk about the *principal* and the *agent*. But this is just shorthand. In agency law, when a lawyer talks about the *principal*, she really means the *principal person* or the *principal actor*.

Homophones like *principle* and *principal* (and others that are less tricky—like *they're, their,* and *there*—but that can still trip up rushed writers), simply need to be added to your editing checklist. Look for them and fix them when they are wrong. It's an easy fix that will significantly improve the clarity of your writing.

Finally, keep in mind, as you are choosing the right word, that the right word should be accurate but should also have the connotation that you intend. Within the range of clear, correct words that accurately convey your meaning, you can select those that best paint the picture you want the reader to see. Has your client spent the past six years in *prison* or in a *correctional facility*? While *prison* might be the most clear and accurate, *correctional facility* might actually be the *right* word.

✍ Editing Strategy 4.3
Check That Language Is Consistent

Once you've chosen the right word, you should, for the most part, stick with it. Now, this isn't great advice for every kind of writing. In fact, in some kinds of writing, writers regularly look to a thesaurus to avoid repeating words too frequently and to help create elegant variation. But this advice — to use language consistently — is crucial for legal writing.

In legal writing, as in many other forms of technical writing, clarity is the principal goal. It is — and this takes a lot of getting used to for many writers — more important than style. So, while elegant variation might feel less dull and monotonous to a writer, it causes problems for legal readers.

Using consistent language is most important when the language you are using is a term of art (see Editing Strategy 4.1) or even just language that courts typically use to describe a rule or a standard in a specific area of the law. One way, then, to be sure that you are using language consistently is to look at the way courts use language. For instance, if you discover as you are reading about negligence that courts typically refer to the *reasonable person*, be sure that you use *reasonable person* in your own writing. You might be tempted to substitute *equitable*, *just*, or *rational* as a way to avoid the repetition of *reasonable*. But it won't work. Lawyers are careful readers, and if you switch from *reasonable person* to *rational person*, your reader will assume that there was a reason for the switch and then spend frustrating amounts of time trying to puzzle out what that difference is.

Using consistent language is important in legal writing generally, not just where terms of art are concerned. Take a look at Example 4.3(a). Notice the shift in language in the draft and how the elimination of that shift improves the clarity of the revised example.

Example 4.3(a)
Sentence revised by replacing elegant variation with consistent language

Draft: The tort of negligence has four **elements**. Because defendant conceded that the last three **factors** have been met, plaintiff must prove only the first **principle**.

Revision: The tort of negligence has four **elements**. Because defendant conceded that the last three **elements** have been met, plaintiff must prove only the first **element**.

Even if *element* and *factor* didn't mean different things, the draft example would still be problematic for a careful reader. She might ultimately decide that the shift in language didn't mean anything, but she could never be completely certain of the writer's intention. This uncertainty and ambiguity cause problems and affect clarity. But the good news is that the uncertainty and ambiguity are easily fixed — simply replace elegant variation with consistent language.

✍ Editing Strategy 4.4
Check for Ambiguous Pronouns

Choosing words carefully isn't always just a matter of choosing language that's clear, accurate, and consistent. Sometimes it's a matter of grammar.

There are several grammatical problems that can have a real impact on the clarity of writing, but pronoun problems probably top the list. Both this and the next two editing strategies deal with identifying pronoun problems. Of course, to find pronoun problems, you have to start first with finding pronouns.

Grammar Reminder

An **antecedent** is the noun that a pronoun refers to.

A pronoun is a word used in place of a noun that has already been mentioned. That noun that's already been mentioned is called an AN-TECEDENT. The job of the pronoun, then, is to stand in for the antecedent so that the writer doesn't have to continuously repeat it. (See how *it* stands in for *antecedent* in this sentence? Nice, right?)

Express or Implied Antecedent

Lawyers are fond of things being express or implied: express or implied warranties, contracts, consent. But writers should be wary of implication, especially when it comes to antecedents.

In writing, especially clear legal writing, antecedents need to be express, they need to be nouns, and they need to come before the pronouns that are replacing them.

You might be tempted to write: "***It*** did not address the second issue because the court's conclusion on the first issue settled the matter." Avoid the temptation. This sentence breaks all the rules. The antecedent (*the court*) is implied (in the phrase *the court's conclusion*) and isn't even a noun at all. And finally, the antecedent shows up after the noun.

While your reader will probably figure out what you mean, she won't be happy to work that hard for a sentence that could have been more clearly written in the first place. So, fix the sentence by making the subject that was implied — the court — express. Then, put it in the sentence before the pronoun. "The court did not address the second issue because its conclusion on the first issue settled the matter."

There are actually quite a few different kinds of pronouns. Chart 4.4 lists pronouns by category. While you certainly don't need to memorize each of the categories, the chart will give you a sense of the pretty wide variety.

Chart 4.4
Pronouns

Personal Pronouns
       Singular: I, me, you, she, her, he, him, it
       Plural: we, us, you, they, them

Possessive Pronouns
       Singular: my, mine, your, yours, her, hers, his, its
       Plural: our, ours, your, yours, their, theirs

Intensive and Reflexive Pronouns
       Singular: myself, yourself, himself, herself, itself
       Plural: ourselves, yourselves, themselves

Relative Pronouns
       Who, whom, whose, which, that

Interrogative Pronouns
       Who, whom, whose, which, that

Demonstrative Pronouns
       This, that, these, those

Indefinite Pronouns

all	anything	another	everything
somebody	anybody	no one	something
each	both	neither	some
everyone	nobody	anyone	either
someone	everybody	nothing	

Reciprocal Pronouns
       Each other, one another

Pronouns are wonderful because they allow writers to avoid the monotony of continuously repeating the noun (remember, grammarians call it the antecedent). Take a look at Example 4.4(a). Notice how the revision, which includes pronouns, is so much easier to read than the draft, which doesn't.

Example 4.4(a)
Sentence revised by replacing nouns with pronouns

Draft: In *McCallen*, the court held that the claimant, MacDonald, did not have an opportunity to withdraw from a physical fight with MacDonald's foreman. *Id.*

> MacDonald was angry that MacDonald's foreman used MacDonald's truck, so MacDonald engaged the foreman in a heated debate. *Id.* at 741. The foreman grabbed MacDonald, MacDonald and the foreman struggled for a moment, and MacDonald and the foreman both fell over a chain behind MacDonald's leg, ending the fight. *Id.*
>
> Revision: In *McCallen,* the court held that the claimant, MacDonald, did not have an opportunity to withdraw from a physical fight with **his** foreman. *Id.* MacDonald was angry that **his** foreman used **his** truck, so MacDonald engaged the foreman in a heated debate. *Id.* at 741. The foreman grabbed MacDonald, **they** struggled for a moment, and **they** both fell over a chain behind MacDonald's leg, ending the fight. *Id.*

But, using pronouns doesn't always make writing easier to read. Take, for example, the sentence in Example 4.4(b). This sentence takes pronouns to the extreme in order to avoid repeating any nouns. The result is a jumble of *he* and *him* with absolutely no way of telling who did what.

> **Example 4.4(b)**
> **Ineffective and ambiguous use of pronouns**
>
> Draft: In *McCallen,* the court held that the claimant, MacDonald, did not have an opportunity to withdraw from a physical fight with **his** foreman. *Id.* **He** was angry that **he** used **his** truck, so **he** engaged **him** in a heated debate. *Id.* at 741. **He** grabbed **him, they** struggled for a moment, and **they** both fell over a chain behind **his** leg, ending the fight. *Id.*

Example 4.4(b) demonstrates, albeit in a very exaggerated way, a very common pronoun problem: ambiguous pronouns.

An ambiguous pronoun is any pronoun that lacks a clear antecedent. Take another look at Example 4.4(b). Because MacDonald and his foreman are both male, they both get replaced with the personal pronoun *he* or *him.* So, at some point, it becomes impossible to tell whether *he* is meant to replace MacDonald or MacDonald's foreman. The result: several ambiguous pronoun references.

To find ambiguous pronouns, begin by searching for pronouns. Anytime a pronoun appears, check that it has a clear antecedent. If there are two (or more) possible antecedents, then revise by changing the pronoun back into a noun.

Take a look at Example 4.4(c) and see if you can spot the ambiguous pronoun.

Example 4.4(c)
Sentence with ambiguous pronoun

Draft: The assault was most likely connected to the job assignment because it arose from an argument over a tip.

Did you find the ambiguous pronoun? It was *it*. Notice how, in the sentence in Example 4.4(c), the pronoun *it* could refer to either the noun *assault* or the noun *job assignment*. Because there are two possible antecedents, the pronoun reference is ambiguous.

Now, look at Example 4.4(d), which provides two different ways of revising the ambiguous pronoun in Example 4.4(c).

Example 4.4(d)
Sentence with ambiguous pronoun revised in two different ways

Revision: The assault was most likely connected to the job assignment because the assault arose from an argument over a tip.

Revision: The assault was most likely connected to the job assignment because the claimant's co-worker hit him during an argument over a tip.

The revised sentences offer two possible ways of turning the pronoun back into a noun. The first is to simply restate the antecedent—the *assault*. Another option (which avoids the repetition but also uses inconsistent language) is to turn the pronoun *it* back into a noun but use *hit* instead of *assault* in the second part of the sentence.

Both revisions work; neither revision is necessarily better than the other. Whether to opt for the repetition or risk the inconsistent language is a difficult choice that the writer has to make. (Take another look at When Editing Strategies Compete in Chapter 3. Editing strategies often compete and writers have to make hard choices about which editing strategy to choose.) Here, making that decision simply requires the writer to keep in mind that clarity is the ultimate goal.

✍ Editing Strategy 4.5
Check for Remote Pronouns

Sometimes a pronoun causes problems because it could refer to several different antecedents. Other times, a pronoun causes a problem because it is too far away from its antecedent. This problem—remote pronoun reference—is a bit tricky to find but very easy to fix.

To find a remote pronoun reference that is causing a problem, begin by looking for pronouns. Anytime you see one, take a quick look for the antecedent. (Save time by combining this editing strategy with the last one, and identify both ambiguous pronouns and remote pronoun references at the same time.)

If you have to search back over several sentences to find the antecedent, you probably have a remote pronoun reference. And chances are pretty good that it will cause problems for your reader. Fix the problem by converting the pronoun back into a noun. Most of the time, this is a simple matter of replacing the pronoun with the antecedent.

Unfortunately, there is no good rule about how far is too far when it comes to pronouns and their antecedents. The draft in Example 4.5(a) shows a pronoun just a little too far away from its antecedent.

Example 4.5(a)
Sentence with remote pronoun revised by substituting the antecedent for the pronoun

Draft: By threatening Ms. Green and creating the perception of threat, Mr. Young probably verbally initiated the assault. **His** behavior was most likely threatening. Like the claimant in *Kessen*, **he** approached Ms. Green and angrily addressed her.

Revision: By threatening Ms. Green and creating the perception of threat, Mr. Young probably verbally initiated the assault. **His** behavior was most likely threatening. Like the claimant in *Kessen*, **Mr. Young** approached Ms. Green and angrily addressed her.

Notice how the pronoun *his* in the last sentence is separated from the antecedent—*Mr. Young*—by just one sentence. But even that distance could create momentary confusion for a reader. The revision, which repeats the antecedent, is much easier to read and immediately understand. In other words, it's clearer.

Deciding whether a pronoun is too far away from its antecedent is probably more of an art than a science. Try identifying pronouns that could potentially cause problems. Then, err on the side of caution and fix them.

> ✍ Editing Strategy 4.6
> **Check That Pronouns and Their Antecedents Agree**

Because a pronoun's job is to stand in for a noun — the antecedent — it's important that the pronoun and antecedent agree. Really, this just means that if the antecedent is plural, the pronoun has to be plural. And if the antecedent is singular, the pronoun has to be singular (and also the right gender).

In theory, this is a really easy rule to follow, especially once you've edited out all ambiguous and remote pronouns. Once you've done that editing, you just have to look for the pronoun, find the antecedent, and make sure they match. In Example 4.6(a), the antecedent, MacDonald, is a man and there is only one of him. So, the right pronoun to use is *his* — the male, singular pronoun.

Example 4.6(a)
Sentence with pronoun and antecedent that agree

Revised: In *McCallen,* the court held that the claimant, **MacDonald**, did not have an opportunity to withdraw from a physical fight with **his** foreman. *Id.*

But, while it's an easy rule in theory, there are a couple of traps almost everyone falls into once in a while. The first trap is treating COLLECTIVE NOUNS as if they were plural. Collective nouns are nouns that name a class or a group. *Jury, court, committee,* and *board* are all collective nouns that lawyers write about with some frequency.

Grammar Reminder
A **collective noun** is a noun that names a class or group.

The trick is that, even though a jury is made up of twelve individuals, it really functions as a group. So, when you are choosing a pronoun to stand in for a collective noun, choose a singular pronoun. Example 4.6(b) shows how.

Example 4.6(b)
Sentence with pronoun agreement problems, edited by replacing plural pronoun with singular pronoun

Draft: After deliberating for several hours, the **jury** was unable to reach a unanimous decision. **They** notified the bailiff, who informed the judge.

> Revision: After deliberating for several hours, the **jury** was unable
> to reach a unanimous decision. **It** notified the bailiff,
> who informed the judge.

Notice how in the draft in Example 4.6(b), the collective noun *jury* is treated as if it is plural. But the revision gets it right: the singular pronoun *it* stands in for the collective noun *jury*.

There is one exception to the general rule that collective nouns are treated as singular. If the members of the group are clearly functioning as individuals, then the collective noun should be treated as plural. Example 4.6(c) demonstrates a collective noun being treated as a singular noun. The draft sentence gets it wrong, but either revision would work.

Example 4.6(c)
Sentence where collective noun actually needs to be replaced with a plural pronoun

Draft: The **court** came to a decision but that decision was not unanimous. **It** wrote separate opinions.

Revision: The **court** came to a decision, but that decision was not unanimous. **They** wrote separate opinions.

Revision: The court came to a decision, but that decision was not unanimous. Each justice wrote a separate opinion.

While the correct pronoun for a court is usually *it*, *it* won't work in the sentence in Example 4.6(c) because each justice wrote a separate opinion—the members of this group were clearly functioning as individuals. The first revision makes that clear. Note, however, that the second revision is even stronger. In that revision, the author avoids the pronoun altogether. The result is a clearer sentence.

Another trap is using the plural pronouns *they*, *their*, and *them* to refer to a singular antecedent. Take, for example, the draft sentence in Example 4.6(d).

Example 4.6(d)
Sentence with pronoun agreement problem edited by replacing plural pronoun with singular pronoun

Draft: The **police officer** searched the car. But **they** found nothing.

Revision: The **police officer** searched the car. But **she** found nothing.

Admittedly, Example 4.6(d) is pretty simplistic. Most lawyers wouldn't make that particular mistake. However, it actually is very common for lawyers to make this general mistake. Example 4.6(e) is a much more realistic example of this problem.

Example 4.6(e)
Sentence with plural pronoun incorrectly used with singular antecedent

Draft: A seizure occurs when, in view of all of the surrounding circumstances, a **reasonable person** would have believed that **they** were not free to leave. *U.S. v. Mendenhall*, 446 U.S. 544, 554 (1980).

In Example 4.6(e), the antecedent is *a reasonable person*. Because the antecedent is singular, it requires a singular pronoun.

Finding singular antecedents paired with plural pronouns is really straightforward. Look for the pronoun and then find its antecedent. (Are you beginning to see a pattern here?)

But fixing the problem is a little more difficult. Take another look at Example 4.6(e). The writer of the draft probably chose the plural pronoun because, well, who knows whether a reasonable person is male or female. To avoid using sexist language, the writer just opted for using the plural pronoun. While this might work in spoken language, writers should be more careful. And there are several ways that writers can be more careful.

One fix is to simply get rid of the pronoun and repeat the antecedent. That's the solution that the writer used in Example 4.6(f).

Example 4.6(f)
Sentence with pronoun agreement problems revised by replacing the pronoun with the antecedent

Draft: A seizure occurs when, in view of all of the surrounding circumstances, a **reasonable person** would have believed that **they** were not free to leave. *U.S. v. Mendenhall*, 446 U.S. 544, 554 (1980).

Revision: A seizure occurs when, in view of all of the surrounding circumstances, a **reasonable person** would have believed that **the reasonable person** was not free to leave. *U.S. v. Mendenhall*, 446 U.S. 544, 554 (1980).

Another option is to choose either a masculine or a feminine pronoun and then stick with it. (Some writers choose to alternate between the masculine and feminine. This is another possibility as long as alternating won't cause confusion and impact clarity.) In Example 4.6(g), the writer has chosen the pronoun *she* just because the client in the case—the one who was arguably seized—is a woman.

Example 4.6(g)
Sentence with pronoun agreement problem revised by replacing plural pronoun with a singular pronoun

Draft: A seizure occurs when, in view of all of the surrounding circumstances, a **reasonable person** would have believed that **they** were not free to leave. *U.S. v. Mendenhall*, 446 U.S. 544, 554 (1980).

Revision: A seizure occurs when, in view of all of the surrounding circumstances, a **reasonable person** would have believed that **she** was not free to leave. *U.S. v. Mendenhall*, 446 U.S. 544, 554 (1980).

If choosing a pronoun feels uncomfortable, another option is to use the phrase *he or she* or *him or her*. That's the solution the writer in Example 4.6(h) opted for.

Example 4.6(h)
Sentence with pronoun agreement problem revised by replacing plural pronoun with *he or she*

Draft: A seizure occurs when, in view of all of the surrounding circumstances, a **reasonable person** would have believed that **they** were not free to leave. *U.S. v. Mendenhall*, 446 U.S. 544, 554 (1980).

Revision: A seizure occurs when, in view of all of the surrounding circumstances, a **reasonable person** would have believed that **he or she** was not free to leave. *U.S. v. Mendenhall*, 446 U.S. 544, 554 (1980).

Finally, sometimes, making the antecedent plural or rewriting the sentence to avoid the problem altogether will actually be the best options.

The final pronoun trap is pretty closely related to the first. Just as collective nouns have to be replaced with singular pronouns, INDEFI-NITE PRONOUNS have to be replaced with singular pronouns. To really understand this trap, you have to back up a little bit and understand that antecedents can be nouns or pronouns. That's right. A pronoun can stand in not only for an actual noun but for another pronoun as well. Take a look at Example 4.6(i), where the indefinite pronoun *everyone* is the antecedent.

Grammar Reminder

An **indefinite pronoun** is a pronoun that refers to a nonspecific person or thing (everyone, each).

Example 4.6(i)
Sentence with pronoun agreement problem revised by replacing indefinite pronoun with concrete noun

Draft: The goal of the Fourth Amendment is to protect **everyone** against unreasonable searches of **their** property. *U.S. v. Mendenhall*, 446 U.S. 544, 554 (1980).

Revision: The goal of the Fourth Amendment is to protect **citizens** against unreasonable searches of **their** property. *U.S. v. Mendenhall*, 446 U.S. 544, 554 (1980).

To fix the pronoun problem, the writer of Example 4.6(i) employed the final two strategies suggested above. He rewrote the sentence to avoid using the indefinite pronoun (and resulting pronoun problem) and then used a plural antecedent.

But any of the other strategies suggested above can also work with indefinite pronouns (repeat the antecedent, choose a masculine or feminine pronoun, use the phrase *his or her*), depending upon the circumstances. Ultimately, the goal is to fix the problem thoughtfully, using whatever technique will create the clearest writing.

✍ Editing Strategy 4.7
Check That Subjects and Verbs Agree

Just as pronouns need to agree with their antecedents, subjects need to agree with their verbs: singular nouns need singular verbs and plural nouns need plural verbs. Most of the time, this is incredibly easy to do. In fact, native English speakers do it without a second thought.

But subject-verb agreement is so deceptively simple that even careful writers make mistakes. The first common mistake is to make the verb agree with a noun that appears to be the subject of the sentence but actually isn't.

The reason this mistake is so common is there are often groups of words between the subject and the verb. These word groups usually modify the noun. Remember that modifiers are just words, phrases, or clauses that modify or qualify something (take another look at What is a Modifier Anyway? in Chapter 3), so the modifier could be a dependent clause or a prepositional phrase. The point is, it's not the subject.

In Example 4.7(a), the subject of the sentence is *purposes*, not *requirement*.

> **Example 4.7(a)**
> **Sentence with a prepositional phrase between the subject and verb, revised so the verb agrees with the actual subject of the sentence**
>
> Draft: The **purposes** of the actual notice requirement **is** illustrated in *Shilts v. Young*, 567 P.2d 769, 776 (Alaska 1977).
>
> Revision: The **purposes** of the actual notice requirement **are** illustrated in *Shilts v. Young*, 567 P.2d 769, 776 (Alaska 1977).

To find this problem, identify the subject and verb in the sentence and then make sure they match. Of course, that general guidance will only work if you are identifying the actual subject of the sentence. To do that, try mentally stripping away modifiers so that you can isolate the noun that really is the subject. (In Example 4.7(a), you could rewrite the sentence to say, *The purposes are illustrated …*)

Once you've isolated the noun, ensuring that the subject and verb match will be simple. (Or, you could avoid the problem altogether by checking for too many dependent clauses—Editing Strategy 3.8—or too many prepositional phrases—Editing Strategy 3.9. You'll also go a long way to avoiding the problem by making sure that the subject of the sentence is close to the verb. More on that in Editing Strategy 4.8.)

Grammar Reminder

A **compound subject** is a subject that is made up of two or more simple subjects joined with a coordinating conjunction.

Another common mistake is to pair the wrong verb with a COMPOUND SUBJECT. A compound subject is a subject with two or more parts (the parts are simple subjects—in Example 4.7(b) the two parts are *activities* and *improvement*). If those parts are joined with *and*, treat the subject as plural. But if those parts are joined with *or* or *nor*, make the verb agree with the part of the subject that is nearer to the verb.

Example 4.7(b) demonstrates subject-verb agreement with a compound subject joined with the word *and*.

> **Example 4.7(b)**
> **Sentence with compound subject joined with *and*, revised so that subject is treated as a plural subject**
>
> Draft: The Blys' **activities** on the land **and** the **improvement** they made on the property **demonstrates** that their possession was open and notorious.
>
> Revision: The Blys' **activities** on the land **and** the **improvement** they made on the property **demonstrate** that their possession was open and notorious.

Notice in Example 4.7(b) that because the subject—*activities and improvement*—is plural, the verb should be *demonstrate* not *demonstrates*.

Example 4.7(c) shows subject-verb agreement with a compound subject joined with the word *nor*.

Example 4.7(c)
**Sentence with compound subject joined with *neither . . . nor*
revised so that the verb agrees with the part of the subject that
is singular to the verb**

Draft: Neither the claimant's **activities** on the land **nor her
            reputation** in the community **were** enough to
            demonstrate constructive notice.

Revision: Neither the claimant's **activities** on the land **nor her
            reputation** in the community **was** enough to
            demonstrate constructive notice.

Revision: Neither the claimant's **reputation** in the community **nor
            her activities** on the land **were** enough to demonstrate
            constructive notice.

In Example 4.7(c), the draft sentence is wrong because the part of the subject nearest to the verb—*reputation*—is singular and needs a singular verb. The revisions demonstrate two possible alternatives—changing the verb or rearranging the subject.

Again, the easy way to identify this problem is to carefully identify the subject and verb. If the subject is compound—that is, joined with *and, or,* or *nor*—pay closer attention to the verb you choose.

The final most common mistakes are going to sound really familiar because they showed up first as pronoun problems. But collective nouns and indefinite pronouns are just tricky enough that they deserve another mention.

Remember, collective nouns are singular. This means that, in addition to being replaced by singular pronouns, they also call for singular verbs. (Unless, again this should sound familiar, the meaning is clearly plural.) Example 4.7(d) takes another look at that now-familiar jury example, focusing this time on the verb (which is italicized). Because the jury is a collective noun, it is singular and requires the singular verb.

Example 4.7(d)
**Sentence with collective noun revised so that collective noun is
treated as singular**

Draft: After deliberating for several hours, the **jury** *were*
            unable to reach a unanimous decision.

> Revision: After deliberating for several hours, the **jury** *was* unable
> to reach a unanimous decision.

Finally, remember that indefinite pronouns are also treated as singular. Example 4.7(e) demonstrates how the indefinite pronoun *each* is actually singular and needs a singular verb.

Example 4.7(e)
Sentence with indefinite pronoun revised so that indefinite pronoun is treated as singular

Draft: To acquire property through adverse possession, a claimant must prove that, for ten years, her use of the disputed property was (1) continuous, (2) open and notorious, (3) exclusive, and (4) hostile. *Nome 2000 v. Fagerstrom*, 799 P.2d 304, 309 (Alaska 1990). **Each** of these elements **have** been satisfied in this case.

Revision: To acquire property through adverse possession, a claimant must prove that, for ten years, her use of the disputed property was (1) continuous, (2) open and notorious, (3) exclusive, and (4) hostile. *Nome 2000 v. Fagerstrom*, 799 P.2d 304, 309 (Alaska 1990). **Each** of these elements **has** been satisfied in this case.

---

2. Place Words Carefully

Choosing the right words is important. After agonizing over the perfect word, you still have to put it in the right place. Remember, after you choose the right tool, you have to use it the right way. (Yes, in case you are still wondering, it is next to impossible to fasten a screw with a hammer.)

Most of the time, word placement just isn't an issue. Sure, it's a problem as you are learning a language. If you've ever taken a foreign language class, you might have been surprised to learn that you had to learn a whole new set of rules about where the subject and verb are supposed to go. But, by the time you are fluent in the language, you probably never think about word order or placement.

Even though most aspects of word placement don't require a second thought, there are a few that deserve some special attention. First, subjects and verbs belong close together, so spend a little extra time making sure you keep them close. Second, be sure that you put modifiers where they belong.

✍ Editing Strategy 4.8
Check That Subjects and Verbs Are Close Together

There are some things that you simply can't change about your reader. You just have to accept them and adjust your writing accordingly. Here's one of those things: a reader can't comprehend a sentence until she's read both the subject and the verb. She just can't, no matter how much you might want her to.

The best way to cater to your reader then is to be sure that you keep your subject and verb close together. If you've been making your way diligently through your editing checklist, you might not have any problem here. If you've edited out long sentences—Editing Strategy 3.6—and sentences with too many dependent clauses and prepositional phrases—Editing Strategies 3.8 and 3.9—chances are your subjects and verbs are already pretty close together. But do one more check. It's worth it. Because if your reader can't comprehend your sentence, there's no way your writing is going to be clear.

Take a look at Example 4.8(a). In the draft, the subject—*activities*—is separated from the verb—*differ*—by more than 30 words. The reader is forced to hold onto the subject for way too long before she understands the sentence. The revision pulls that modifier out of the sentence and turns it into its own sentence. The result is that not only are the subject and verb closer together but the sentence is now a reasonable length. (As an added bonus, splitting up the too long sentence allowed the writer to make a more effective comparison.)

Example 4.8(a)
Sentence with subject and verb too far apart, revised by splitting one sentence into three to keep subjects and verbs close together

Draft: **The Blys' activities** on the Fern Ridge property, which include hunting, fishing, camping, bird watching, and hiking several times a year as well as building a rock wall and a fire pit and clearing some land, **differ** markedly from the activities on the property in *Shilts*.

Revision: **The Blys' activities** on the Fern Ridge property **differ** markedly from the activities on the property in *Shilts*. In *Shilts*, the claimant flew over the property ten to fifty times a year, walked the property boundaries once a year, but did not make any improvements to the land. Conversely, the Blys hunt, fish, camp, bird watch, and

> hike on the Fern Ridge property several times a year and
> built rock walls and a fire pit, and cleared land.

The really good news is that finding and fixing this problem goes hand
in hand with several of the other editing strategies.

Simply find the subject and then find the verb. When you've found
the two, you can check that they agree — Editing Strategy 4.7 — and also
check that they are close enough together that the sentence is clear. While
there is no magic number, a sentence where the subject and verb are separated by more than seven or eight words probably needs some attention.
A sentence where the subject and verb are separated by more than 15
words almost definitely needs to be revised.

✍ Editing Strategy 4.9
Check for Misplaced Modifiers

Modifiers are words, phrases, or clauses that describe something.
When modifiers are in the right place, they are extremely effective. (Not
just plain effective, but *extremely* effective.) However, when modifiers
end up in the wrong place, they can wreak havoc on the clarity of your
writing.

Here's the easiest way to think about modifiers: modifiers should be
as close as possible to the word or phrase that they are describing. Now,
this is not the most sophisticated way to think about modifiers. After all,
modifiers can probably appear at some distance from the word or phrase
that they are modifying. The key is that, the bigger the distance, the
greater chance of a misplaced or dangling modifier.

To be sure that modifiers are in the right place, begin by underlining
the modifiers in your sentence. Then, decide which category each modifier falls into — (1) a one-word modifier, (2) a modifier at the beginning
of a sentence, or (3) a modifier in the middle of or at the end of a sentence. Next, circle the word or phrase that you mean for the modifier to
modify. Finally, decide if, given the type of modifier you're using, the
modifier is in the right place. The following guidelines for different types
of modifiers should help.

(1) **One-word modifiers.** Single word modifiers (*only, even, almost,
nearly, just, really, very*) seem at first glance to be so harmless. But these
little guys can jump all over in a sentence and create chaos.

Generally, one-word modifiers should go right before the word or
phrase that they are meant to modify. That means that you need to be

really sure which word or phrase you really want to modify. (Because you circled it, checking to be sure that you've done this right should be a snap.)

Take a look at Example 4.9(a). Notice that there are several draft sentences and that, without knowing what the writer means, it's impossible to determine which draft is right.

Example 4.9(a)
Sentence where placement of one-word modifier changes the sentence's meaning

Draft: The bike messenger **only** called the attorney's office after she failed to file the consent with the court.

Draft: The bike messenger called **only** the attorney's office after she failed to file the consent with the court.

In the first draft sentence, the modifier—*only*—modifies the word right after it—*called*. So the writer is saying that after she failed to file the consent, the only thing the bike messenger did was call the office. She didn't return there or send an email.

In the second draft of the sentence, the modifier is still modifying what comes after it. Only, this time, the phrase that comes after the modifier is *the attorney's office*. So, the writer is saying that the bike messenger called nowhere but the office. She didn't try the attorney at home or on his cell phone.

The real trick with the misplaced one-word modifier is that a misplaced one-word modifier isn't wrong. Both the sentences in Example 4.9(a) are perfectly grammatical and perfectly logical. They just mean different things. The fact that a one-word modifier can change the entire meaning of a sentence, however, means that you must be even more careful to put those one-word modifiers in the right place.

(2) A modifier at the beginning of a sentence. A modifier that comes at the beginning of a sentence needs to modify the word or phrase right after it. Or maybe it's more accurate to say that a modifier that comes at the beginning of a sentence *will* modify the word or phrase that comes right after it, whether you mean it to or not. So, that word or phrase better be the right one. (Remember you've got that *right* word circled. Be sure that it shows up right after the modifier.)

In the draft sentence in Example 4.9(b), the modifier is misplaced.

Example 4.9(b)
Sentence with misplaced modifier revised so that the modifier comes directly before the noun it is meant to modify

Draft: **After sampling the salad dressing,** the stomach pains that Mrs. Carter described in her complaint began.

Revision: **After sampling the salad dressing,** Mrs. Carter began to experience the stomach pains that she later described in her complaint.

Notice how, in the draft in Example 4.9(b), the modifier—*after sampling the salad dressing*—mistakenly modifies *the stomach pains*. The result is that stomach pains were sampling salad dressing. Strange. What the writer really meant was for the modifier to describe Mrs. Carter. The revision reflects the real meaning.

Example 4.9(c) isn't quite as funny as Example 4.9(b), but it is just as confusing.

Example 4.9(c)
Sentence with misplaced modifier revised so that the modifier is before the noun that it is meant to modify

Draft: **When he returned on October 9,** the secretary had not filed Mr. Alter's consent with the court.

Revision: **When he returned on October 9,** Mr. Alter discovered that the secretary had not filed the consent with the court.

The draft seems to say that the secretary returned on October 9th and had not yet filed the consent. But the revision makes the writer's meaning clear—Mr. Alter was the one returning from vacation on October 9 to the troubling discovery that the secretary hadn't filed the consent.

By underlining the modifier in the earlier draft sentences and then circling the word or phrase that the modifier was meant to describe, the writer would have discovered her mistake. And fixing the misplaced modifiers in those sentences would go a long way toward achieving clarity.

(3) **A modifier in the middle of or at the end of a sentence.** Unlike a modifier that comes at the beginning of a sentence, a modifier that comes in the middle of or at the end of a sentence needs to modify the word or phrase that comes directly *before* it. Again, underline the modifier and circle the word or phrase that it is meant to describe in order to discover any modifiers that are out of place.

In Example 4.9(d), the modifier is misplaced and could be fixed in at least two different ways.

Example 4.9(d)
Sentence with misplaced modifier in the middle of the sentence revised so that the modifier follows the noun it is meant to modify

Draft: The secretary at the office, **who was unaware that the filing deadline had passed**, failed to tell Mr. Alter that the consent had not been filed.

Revision: The secretary, **who was unaware that the filing deadline had passed**, failed to tell Mr. Alter that the consent had not been filed.

Revision: The secretary, **who was at the office and unaware that the filing deadline had passed**, failed to tell Mr. Alter that the consent had not been filed.

Remember that a modifier in the middle of a sentence modifies the word or phrase that comes directly before it. So, in the draft sentence in Example 4.9(d), the modifier—*who was unaware that the filing deadline had passed*—seems to be modifying the prepositional phrase *at the office*. But that's not right. The modifier is supposed to be describing the secretary. (While the modifier could arguably be referring to the entire phrase *the secretary at the office*, it seems silly to argue over the meaning when the sentence can be so easily fixed.) The writer could rewrite the draft sentences in a few different ways, depending on what information she wants the sentence to convey. The two revisions in Example 4.9(d) demonstrate a couple of possibilities.

Modifiers at the end of a sentence can cause just as much confusion. Take a look at Example 4.9(e).

Example 4.9(e)
Sentence with misplaced modifier at the end of the sentence revised so the modifier follows the noun it is meant to modify

Draft: She left the office with fifteen minutes to reach the courthouse, **which was normally plenty of time.**

Revision: She left the office for the courthouse fifteen minutes before the consent needed to be filed. Normally, fifteen minutes is plenty of time to make the trip from the office to the courthouse.

In Example 4.9(e) the draft sentence seems to be suggesting that the courthouse is *normally plenty of time*. But that doesn't make any sense. Sure, the reader will figure out what the writer meant. But the reader shouldn't have to mentally rewrite the sentence. Rewriting is the writer's job.

Again, identifying both the modifier and the word or phrase that it's meant to modify will help you to see misplaced modifiers that can easily slip past you when you read what you meant rather than what you actually wrote.

Ignoring and Breaking Grammar Rules

When you write, it's a good idea to follow grammar rules most of the time. Sometimes, however, you should ignore or even break grammar rules.

First, ignore grammar rules when using them results in awkwardness. In other words, don't do something that is technically grammatically correct if it has a negative impact on your writing. This can definitely happen with modifiers.

For example, you might say, "The attorney, in an effort to avoid the traffic caused by the heat and rolling blackouts, used a bicycle messenger to file the notice of removal with the court." That sentence is technically correct. The modifier, which is in the middle of the sentence, comes right after the noun that it meant to modify. The sentence is correct. But it is also awkward at least in part because the subject and verb are way too far apart.

To fix this correct but awkward sentence, move the modifier. "In an effort to avoid the traffic caused by the heat and rolling blackouts, the attorney used a bicycle messenger to file the notice of removal with the court." By moving the modifier, you're able to create a sentence that is grammatically correct and avoids the awkwardness in the sample sentence.

Second, break grammar rules that aren't actually grammar rules. The reality is that the English language evolves and some rules are no longer rules. For example, you may at one time have been told that you should never split an infinitive. (If you have never heard this advice, then you may need to know that an infinitive consists of *to* plus a verb — *to write, to read, to teach*.) But most experts actually encourage writers to split infinitives sometimes. For instance, it sounds awkward to say, "The bike messenger decided to avoid traffic carefully." Instead, say, "The bike messenger decided to carefully avoid traffic." You've split the infinitive *to avoid*, but you've written a clearer sentence in the process.

✍ Editing Strategy 4.10
Check for Dangling Modifiers

When you are looking for misplaced modifiers, you'll also be able to spot dangling modifiers. A dangling modifier is a modifier that doesn't actually refer to any word or phrase in the sentence. Dangling modifiers often hint at what they're modifying. But don't take for granted that your reader will pick up on your hint. Instead, anytime you identify a modifier, be sure that it's actually modifying something. (That same technique to "underline the modifier, circle the word or phrase that it's modifying" will work here. It's just that, when you go to circle that word or phrase, it won't be there.)

In Example 4.10(a), the draft sentence begins with a dangling modifier and, as a result, is difficult to follow.

Example 4.10(a)
Sentence with dangling modifier revised by explicitly stating the noun that the modifier is meant to modify

Draft: **In an effort to avoid the traffic,** the consent to the court was delivered by bike messenger.

Revision: **In an effort to avoid the traffic,** the attorney used a bike messenger to deliver the consent to the court.

Notice how, in Example 4.10(a), the sentence begins with a modifier—*in an effort to avoid the traffic.* But the noun that that modifier is meant to describe—*the attorney*—is absent, obscured by the use of passive voice. The revision fixes the dangling modifier by restoring the noun to the sentence. The modifier now has something to modify.

Sometimes a dangling modifier is hard to spot because, at first glance, it seems to be modifying something. Take Example 4.10(b). At first glance, the draft sentence seems to work.

Example 4.10(b)
Sentence with dangling modifier revised by explicitly stating the noun that the modifier is meant to modify

Draft: **Upon entering the intersection,** the messenger's bike was hit by a car.

Revision: **When the bike messenger entered the intersection,** her bike was hit by a car.

But slow down and look a little more closely at the draft sentence in Example 4.10(b). Certainly the messenger's bike didn't make its way into the intersection all by itself. While the phrase *the messenger's bike* hints at the noun that is supposed to be modified—*the messenger*—hinting is not enough. The revision makes the writer's meaning clear.

While finding a dangling modifier can sometimes be tricky, fixing this mistake generally is not. To fix a dangling modifier, simply revise the sentence so that the word or phrase that the modifier is meant to modify actually shows up in the sentence.

✎ Editing Strategy 4.11
Check for Squinting Modifiers

The final modifier problem that you're likely to come upon when you're searching for misplaced modifiers is the squinting modifier. A squinting modifier is a modifier that is sitting between two things that it could possibly modify. If a modifier could modify two different things, the reader is forced to make a decision about which one it actually modifies. So, the modifier isn't exactly misplaced, but it's still causing a problem.

Squinting modifiers probably occur less frequently than misplaced or dangling modifiers. However, doing a quick check for squinting modifiers while you are checking for misplaced and dangling modifiers is probably still worth your while.

In the draft in Example 4.11(a), the modifier—*quickly*—is sitting right between the verb *pedaling* and the verb *fell*.

Example 4.11(a)
Sentence with squinting modifier revised so that the modifier is clearly modifying a single verb

Draft: The bike messenger who was pedaling **quickly** fell when the car struck her.

Revised: The bike messenger was pedaling **quickly** but fell when the car struck her.

The modifier in the draft is squinting because it could potentially modify either *pedaling* or *fell*. Either the messenger was pedaling quickly or she fell quickly. To fix this squinting modifier, the writer needs to decide which verb the modifier is meant to describe and then do a bit of rearranging. The revision sentence provides one possibility.

Clear Writing:
The Exercises

1. Choose Words Carefully

Use Editing Strategies 4.1 through 4.7 to edit the following passage from the memo on burglary.

In *Nollen*, the court found that a semi-truck trailer was a building because it had been adapted for use as a business. *Id.* St. Vincent de Paul, a charitable organization, utilized the semi-truck trailer as a donation center. *Id.* at 788. A truck would tow a trailer to the transfer station, but then the driver would detach the trailer and leave it until such time as the truck was procured by St. Vincent. *Id.* In addition to the driver leaving the trailer for a period of time, they placed a temporary stairway next to the trailer so that members of the public could walk up the stairs and into the trailer to make their donations. *Id.* St. Vincent also placed permanent signs besides trailer advertising it as a donation collection station. *Id.* According to the court, by effectuating these changes, it had changed the trailer from its ordinary use as a vehicle to use in the business of collecting and redistributing donations. *Id.* at 789. The court believed that, as the statute does not require that the conversion of a vehicle be permanent, the changes to the trailer were sufficient even though the trailer was not permanently located at the transfer station. *Id.* at 145. Thus, the trailer was a building. *Id.*

On the other hand, in *State v. Scott*, 590 P.2d 743, 744 (Or. App. 1979), the court argued that a railroad boxcar was not a building because it had not been modified to be used as anything other then a vehicle. In *Scott*, the defendant entered a railroad boxcar with the intent to commit a crime. *See id.* However, because the railroad boxcar was not a building, the court overturned his burglary conviction. *Id.* The court felt that a boxcar could conceivably be prepared for business. *Id.* However, as the boxcar in that case had not been changed in any way from its ordinary purpose — that is, because it was still simply a "structure on wheels designed for the storage of goods and their transportation" — the court found that it was not a building. *Id.*

2. Place Words Carefully

Use Editing Strategies 4.8 through 4.11 to edit the following passage from the memo on burglary.

Here, the mobile bakery that Mr. Dennison entered is a building because it has been adapted for carrying on business. The mobile bakery, which was originally simply a utility van, has been changed and modified, much in the same way that the trailer in *Nollen* was modified and stands in contrast to the boxcar in *Scott*. Like in *Nollen*, which was detached from the truck that towed it, the van's awning was open and extending from the side of the van and chairs were positioned under that awning. These changes make both the trailer in *Nollen* and the mobile bakery unsuitable for use as a vehicle while they are in business. But Ms. Carlson has made even more changes to the van and to her business practices, which make it markedly different from the boxcar in *Scott*. Unlike in *Scott*, where there was no evidence that the boxcar had been modified at all, there is ample evidence of modifications to the van. Ms. Carlson put down laminate flooring and added refrigerator space for her products and added a sink and small bathroom. All of these changes demonstrate that the van has been adapted for a new purpose.

Moreover, the changes to the mobile bakery make it suitable for use in a commercial or industrial enterprise. In other words, the van, like the truck in *Nollen* but unlike the boxcar in *Scott*, is suitable for use as a business. Just like St. Vincent's approach, which placed stairs next to the donation truck so that patrons could enter the trailer and leave their donations, Ms. Carlson opens the van doors and the side window to create a service counter, and she opens the awning at the side of the van so that patrons can relax in chairs in its shade. In addition, like St. Vincent advertising the trailer as the location of its business, Ms. Carlson advertises the mobile bakery as the location of her business. St. Vincent de Paul placed permanent signs near the trailer advertising it as a donation center. While Ms. Carlson has no permanent signs to advertise her van as a mobile bakery, there are display signs listing the cupcake flavors and prices, and she plays music from a portable speaker. Both the temporary cupcake signs and the music serve a similar purpose to the St. Vincent's permanent signs — advertising a business. In fact, the changes that Ms. Carlson made to the van are presumably the kinds of changes that the court in *Scott* alluded to when it suggested that a vehicle could conceivably be modified so that it could be used for business purposes. Ms. Carlson's van is now much more than just a "structure on wheels designed for the storage of goods and their transportation." Through the changes, it has become suitable for use as a business and thus is a building. Unlike the lack of changes to the railroad boxcar in *Scott* and like the changes to the trailer in *Nollen*, the changes to the mobile bakery adapted the vehicle from its ordinary use for transportation to use in Ms. Carlson's bakery business.

However, Mr. Dennison may argue that the changes Ms. Carlson made to the mobile cupcake van were not as significant as the changes made to the detached trailer in *Nollen*. He may argue that, unlike the trailer in *Nollen*, which was detached from the truck, the van continued to be really a vehicle. However, because there is no statutory requirement that the adaptation of the vehicle be permanent, this argument is unlikely to succeed. So even though the van might have occasionally been simply transportation like the railroad car in *Scott*, while it was parked and doing business as a mobile bakery, it was a building.

Chapter 5

Polished Writing

"Proper punctuation is both the sign and the cause of clear thinking." — Lynne Truss

The final stage of editing is polishing. Many people mistake polishing for editing and rewriting. They write a single draft, hit print, and do a quick proofread. But this stage — polishing — doesn't make any sense until the others are finished. Your writing should be coherent, vigorous, and clear. Once it is, you are ready to polish.

Although polishing is the last step, it is just as important as the other steps in the editing process. In almost all legal writing, you are asking the reader to trust and believe you. You will make it easier for that reader to trust and believe you if you are careful about every detail, including little details like comma placement and spelling.

When you are not careful about a little detail, like where an apostrophe belongs, your reader will begin to doubt whether you were careful about other, bigger things. And then your reader will start to question whether she can really trust and believe you. And if your reader starts to question whether she can trust and believe you, then all of your hard work has been for nothing.

Even if your reader doesn't follow this slippery slope to complete mistrust, she is still likely to be annoyed that you put an apostrophe where it doesn't belong. Either way, you are much better off if your writing is polished.

While polishing is a straightforward process of checking your grammar, spelling, and punctuation, it is not necessarily an easy process. And it is inevitably time-consuming. So, leave yourself plenty of time to check for little mistakes that could mean big problems for your credibility.

Polished Writing:
The Editing Checklist

1. Check Your Grammar

✍ 5.1 Check for Sentence Fragments

Check that every sentence has a verb and a subject and can stand alone as a complete sentence. If any sentence is missing a verb or a subject or can't stand on its own as a complete sentence, it is a sentence fragment. Fix it by supplying the verb or the subject or pulling the fragment into a nearby sentence.

✍ 5.2 Check for Parallel Structure

Check that parallel ideas are expressed in parallel grammatical form. If they're not, fix them.

✍ 5.3 Check Verb Tense

Check that you've used the right tense for rules and for illustrating cases. Check also that you are familiar with the verb tense conventions of legal writing.

2. Check Your Spelling

✍ 5.4 Check for Tricky Homophones

Check for words that are spelled right but used wrong. Fix them.

✍ 5.5 Just Check

Carefully proofread your writing rather than relying on spell check. While spell check will catch misspelled words, it won't always catch typos.

3. Check Your Punctuation

✍ 5.6 Check Commas

Check that you've used commas where they're necessary and only where they're necessary. Knowing the five most common rules of commas will help.

✍ 5.6-1. Use a comma and a coordinating conjunction to join independent clauses

✍ 5.6-2. Use a comma after an introductory clause or phrase

✍ 5.6-3. Use a comma between all items in a series

✍️ **5.6-4. Use a comma between coordinate adjectives**

✍️ **5.6-5. Use a comma to set off nonrestrictive elements**

✍️ **5.7 Check Semicolons**

Check that you've chosen a semicolon rather than a comma where appropriate.

✍️ **5.7-1. Use a semicolon to join independent clauses**

✍️ **5.7-2. Use a semicolon between items in a series containing internal punctuation**

✍️ **5.8 Check Colons**

Check that you've used colons to tell readers to pay attention to lists and quotations. Make sure that the colon follows an independent clause.

✍️ **5.9 Check Quotation Marks**

Check that you've used quotation marks correctly and that you've punctuated them perfectly.

✍️ **5.10 Check Apostrophes**

Check that you've used apostrophes to signal omissions in contractions and to signal ownership or possession.

4. Polishing and Perfection

Polished Writing:
The Details

1. Check Your Grammar

If you've done a careful job of rewriting — particularly of making your writing clear — then you've already caught some of the most common grammatical mistakes (misplaced modifiers, ambiguous pronouns, subject and verbs that don't agree). But there are still a few other common grammatical mistakes that you should have on your editing checklist. This chapter lists a few, but you should always be on the lookout for other grammar problems in your writing. If you are lucky, you will have a teacher or editor who is willing to point out grammatical mistakes. Don't take this luck for granted. Use that criticism to add to your own editing checklist so that you are editing for the grammatical problems that are most likely to surface in your writing.

✍ Editing Strategy 5.1
Check for Sentence Fragments

One of the most fundamental rules of grammar is that sentences must be complete. To be complete, a sentence must have at least one full independent clause. Remember that an independent clause contains a subject and a verb and either can, or does, stand alone.

When a sentence is incomplete, it is a sentence fragment and must be fixed. Fixing a sentence fragment is actually a pretty easy thing to do. Surprisingly, though, finding a sentence fragment can be difficult, especially when it is nestled in the midst of a handful of complete sentences. Take a look at Example 5.1(a), and see if you can find the sentence fragment(s).

Example 5.1(a)
Paragraph with (unidentified) sentence fragments

Draft: Mr. Young and Ms. Green were friends and roommates, who also worked at the same restaurant. On the night of the assault, Ms. Green was serving in her usual section. On the deck overlooking the water. Mr. Young and Mr. Tull were serving inside. Ms. Green had been waiting on a couple for nearly three hours when she left to take a break. Mr. Young filled in for Ms. Green, and the couple left a few minutes later, leaving a $100.00 tip. And thanking Mr. Young for the excellent service. Mr.

> Young took the money and gave Ms. Green half of the tip. However, when several waiters are involved in the service, the primary waiter normally takes the tip and decides how to split it. Although that is not a formal policy.

You may have spotted the sentence fragments easily. But if you relied on the old editing trick of reading the paragraph aloud, listening for anything that sounded wrong, you may not have been able to identify the sentence fragments at all. Listening for the incomplete sentence won't work because your ear will often simply attach the fragment to another sentence to make it all work. Relying on your computer's grammar checker won't work, either. Grammar checkers won't identify all of the sentence fragments in that paragraph.

Take another look at the paragraph from the last example. This time, in Example 5.1(b), the sentence fragments are in bold. Are you surprised to discover that there were actually three sentence fragments in that short paragraph?

Example 5.1(b)
Paragraph with sentence fragments identified

Draft: Mr. Young and Ms. Greens were friends and roommates, who also worked at the same restaurant. On the night of the assault, Ms. Green was serving in her usual section. **On the deck overlooking the water.** Mr. Young and Mr. Tull were serving inside. Ms. Green had been waiting on a couple for nearly three hours when she left to take a break. Mr. Young filled in for Ms. Green, and the couple left a few minutes later, leaving a $100.00 tip. **And thanking Mr. Young for the excellent service.** Mr. Young took the money and gave Ms. Green half of the tip. However, when several waiters are involved in the service, the primary waiter normally takes the tip and decides how to split it. **Although that is not a formal policy.**

So, rather than listening for the sentence fragment (or relying on your computer's grammar checker), use the following test to decide if your sentence isn't really a sentence at all. First, check to be sure that the sentence has a verb. If it doesn't, then it's a fragment. Look at Example 5.1(c); you'll see how easy it actually is to write a sentence that doesn't have a verb in it.

Example 5.1(c)
Sentence fragment — missing verb

Draft: On the night of the assault, Ms. Green was serving in
            her usual section of the restaurant. **On the deck
            overlooking the water.**

If the sentence does have a verb, check to be sure that the sentence also
has a subject. If it doesn't, it's a fragment. Writing a sentence with no
subject is easier to do than you might think. Take a look at Example
5.1(d). While there is a person in the sentence — *Mr. Young* — there is no
subject. How can you tell? There's no one doing the action — *thanking
Mr. Young.*

Example 5.1(d)
Sentence fragment — missing subject

Draft: Mr. Young filled in for Ms. Green and the couple left a
            few minutes later, leaving a $100.00 tip. **And thanking
            Mr. Young for the excellent service.**

Even if a sentence has both a subject and a verb, you must still do one
final check. You must check to see whether the sentence can stand alone
or whether it's merely a dependent clause (see Editing Strategy 3.8). Look
at Example 5.1(e). Notice how the sentence fragment has both a subject
(*that*) and a verb (*is*), but notice too that the sentence can't actually stand
on its own. Because the sentence begins with the subordinating conjunction *although*, it *depends* on the first sentence for its full meaning and
thus is a *dependent* clause. (If you don't see why this sentence can't actually stand on its own, go back one more time to Editing Strategy 3.8 and
read a bit more about dependent clauses.)

Example 5.1(e)
Sentence fragment — dependent clause

Draft: However, when several waiters are involved in the
            service, the primary waiter normally takes the tip and
            decides how to split it. **Although that is not a formal
            policy.**

Once you've identified a sentence fragment, you can fix it by either at-
taching it to a nearby sentence or turning it into its very own sentence.

Where the problem is a missing verb, you can either pull the fragment
into a nearby sentence, as in the first revision in Example 5.1(f), or turn

the fragment into a complete sentence by supplying the verb, as in the second revision in Example 5.1(f).

Example 5.1(f)
Sentence fragment with missing verb revised by incorporating the fragment into a nearby sentence or, alternately, supplying the verb

Draft:	On the night of the assault, Ms. Green was serving in her usual section of the restaurant. **On the deck overlooking the water.**
Revision:	On the night of the assault, Ms. Green was serving in her usual section of the restaurant on the deck overlooking the water.
Second Revision:	On the night in question, Ms. Green was serving in her usual section of the restaurant. She was serving on the deck overlooking the water.

Where the problem is a missing subject, you also have the option of pulling the fragment into a nearby sentence—the first revision in 5.1(g)—or supplying a subject to create a full sentence—the second revision in 5.1(g).

Example 5.1(g)
Sentence fragment with missing subject revised by incorporating the fragment into a nearby sentence or, alternately, supplying the subject

Draft:	Mr. Young filled in for Ms. Green, and the couple left a few minutes later, leaving a $100.00 tip. **And thanking Mr. Young for the excellent service.**
Revision:	Ms. Young filled in for Ms. Green, and the couple left a few minutes later, leaving a $100.00 tip and thanking Mr. Young for the excellent service.
Second Revision:	Mr. Young filled in for Ms. Green, and the couple left a few minutes later, leaving a $100.00 tip. The couple also thanked Mr. Young for the excellent service.

Finally, if the sentence is a fragment because it's really a dependent clause or phrase, you can fix the fragment by pulling it into the nearby sentence that it depends on, as in the first revision in Example 5.1(h). Or you can delete the language that's causing the problem—the subordinating conjunction *although* in this case—as in the second revision in Example 5.1(h).

Example 5.1(h)
Dependent clause sentence fragment revised by incorporating dependent clause into a nearby sentence or, alternately, making the dependent clause independent

Draft: However, when several waiters are involved in the service, the primary waiter normally takes the tip and decides how to split it. **Although that is not a formal policy.**

Revision: However, when several waiters are involved in the service, the primary waiter normally takes the tip and decides how to split it, even though that is not a formal policy.

Second   However, when several waiters are involved in the
Revision: service, the primary waiter normally takes the tip and decides how to split it. Leaving the decision to the primary server is not a formal policy.

✍ Editing Strategy 5.2
Check for Parallel Structure

Not only do readers expect for sentences to be complete, but readers also have a lot of other expectations when it comes to grammar. The more you can do to meet those expectations, the better your writing will be.

One expectation that most readers share is that parallel ideas will be expressed in parallel grammatical form. While this sounds a bit intimidating, it simply means that, when you make a list, everything in that list should look the same. (Okay, true grammarians know that balancing parallel ideas is a bit more sophisticated than that. And authors know that using parallel structure can be a great way of emphasizing a point. But making a list look the same will go a very long way to meeting reader expectations when it comes to parallel structure.)

You should make your lists look the same in two important ways. First, if you are listing words (*bat, ball*), then everything in the list should be a word. If you are listing phrases (*swinging the bat, catching the ball*), then everything in the list should be a phrase, and if you are listing clauses (*she swung the bat, he caught the ball*), everything in the list should be a clause. Take a look at examples 5.2(a) through (c). Notice how in the draft sentences, something just doesn't seem quite right. In the revision sentences, though, the writer has balanced her lists—words with words, phrases with phrases, and clauses with clauses.

In the draft sentence in Example 5.2(a), the writer has paired a list of words (*a broken jaw* and *a cracked rib*) with a phrase (*got a mild concussion*). The revision sentence fixes this by describing all three injuries with simple words.

Example 5.2(a)
Sentence revised to create a parallel list of words

Draft: In the brief altercation, Mr. Young sustained a broken jaw, a cracked rib, and got a mild concussion.

Revision: In the brief altercation, Mr. Young sustained a broken jaw, a cracked rib, and a mild concussion.

Viewed another way, the draft sentence in Example 5.2(a) might be awkward because a single word (*a cracked rib*) has found its way into a list of phrases (*sustained a broken jaw* and *got a mild concussion*). In Example 5.2(b), the writer fixes the sentence by creating a list of phrases.

Example 5.2(b)
Sentence revised to create a parallel list of phrases

Draft: In the brief altercation, Mr. Young sustained a broken jaw, a cracked rib, and got a mild concussion.

Revision: In the brief altercation, Mr. Young sustained a broken jaw, suffered a cracked rib, and got a mild concussion.

In the draft sentence in Example 5.2(c), the writer has paired a clause (in number one) with two phrases (in number two and three). In the revision, all three parts of the test are expressed in clauses.

Example 5.2(c)
Sentence revised to create a parallel list of clauses

Draft: A court has further clarified this statutory exclusion into a three-part test: (1) the person must be an active participant in the assault, (2) which must not be connected to the job assignment, and (3) which must be a deviation from customary duties. *Kessen v. Boise Cascade Corp.*, 693 P.2d 52, 53 (Or. App. 1984).

> Revision: A court has further clarified this statutory exclusion into a three-part test: (1) the person must be an active participant in the assault, (2) the assault must not be connected to the job assignment, and (3) the assault must be a deviation from customary duties. *Kessen v. Boise Cascade Corp.*, 693 P.2d 52, 53 (Or. App. 1984).

In addition to balancing the list, you should be sure that everything in the list is in parallel grammatical form. Again, this probably sounds more complicated than it is. To put a list into parallel grammatical form, you simply need to be sure that everything in the list (1) is a noun (2) uses the *-ing* form or (3) begins with a verb. Take a look at Examples 5.2(d) through (f). Again, you'll notice that the draft sentences just seem a bit awkward while the revision sentences are easy to read.

In Example 5.2(d), the draft pairs two nouns (*aggressive stance* and *tone of voice*) with an *-ing* form (*being angry*). The revision cleans it up by turning all three things on the list into nouns.

Example 5.2(d)
Sentence revised so all items are nouns

Draft: Mr. Young took an aggressive role in the assault through his aggressive stance, his tone of voice, and by being angry.

Revision: Mr. Young took an aggressive role in the assault through his aggressive stance, his tone of voice, and his apparent anger.

In Example 5.2(e), the revision sentence fixes the awkwardness in the draft by using *-ing* forms for all of the items in the list of Mr. Young's sins.

Example 5.2(e)
Sentence revised so all items are in *-ing* form

Draft: When she confronted Mr. Young, Ms. Green accused him of lying about money, failing to pay the rent, and that he needed to clean up after himself.

Revision: When she confronted Mr. Young, Ms. Green accused him of lying about money, failing to pay the rent, and being a slob.

In Example 5.2(f), the draft sentence pairs two verbs (*cornering* and *speaking*) with an adjective (*threatening*) and a noun (*hand gesture*). The sentence is a bit awkward, but the awkwardness is hard to pinpoint. All three are *-ing* words aren't they? The revision fixes this awkwardness by including a final verb (*using*).

Example 5.2(f)
Sentence revised so all items are verbs

Draft: By cornering Ms. Green, speaking her name in anger, and with a threatening hand gesture, Mr. Young verbally incited an immediate physical response from Ms. Green.

Revision: By cornering Ms. Green, speaking her name in anger, and using a threatening hand gesture, Mr. Young verbally incited an immediate physical response from Ms. Green.

Because your main goal is to be sure that you have parallel grammatical structure anytime you are listing parallel ideas, the easiest way to check for parallel grammatical structures is to look for commas. Anytime you see a comma, you just may have written a list. Check that list to be sure it is in parallel grammatical structure so that you are sure to meet the reader's expectation.

Editing Strategy 5.3
Check Verb Tense

Another grammar check that you'll have to do separately is checking that you've used the right verb tense. While this is something that you've undoubtedly been doing your whole life without even thinking about it — describing things that occurred in the past in past tense and describing things that are occurring in the present in the present tense — when you begin writing in any discipline, you have to pay attention to that discipline's conventions. As it turns out, legal writing has some specific conventions when it comes to verb tenses.

The first convention is that shifts in verb tense are actually okay sometimes. Now, this will probably surprise you because when you were in elementary school, your teacher taught you that you were supposed to maintain a consistent verb tense. She corrected you anytime you began a paragraph or sentence in the past tense and then suddenly, and distractingly, moved to the present tense. (Remember, you wrote: "Yesterday, I played in the yard by myself when suddenly my sister jumps out of the bushes to scare me." Your teacher then corrected you: "No, you began your sentence in the past tense — *played* — so you can't shift to present tense — *jumps*. You must keep your verb tense consistent!")

But, in legal writing, the convention is to talk about legal rules, which describe the current state of the law, in present tense while talking about the cases themselves in the past tense. This convention can result in tense shifts within a single paragraph. Take a look at Example 5.3(a). Notice that the first sentence, which describes the rule or principle, is written in the present tense while the description of the case itself is written in the past tense. The verbs are in bold so that you can easily see this shift in tense.

Example 5.3(a)
Paragraph with a shift of verb tense

Revision: A building **is** not a dwelling when it **is** not intermittently occupied at night. *State v. Eaton*, 602 P.2d 1159, 1160 (Or. App. 1979). The building in *Eaton* **was located** at a church camp and campers **occupied** it for just eight weeks each summer. *Id.* The rest of the year, the building **remained** empty. *Id.*

While this tense shift might be irritating to your elementary school teacher or your high school English teacher—more on that in a minute—it is the kind of shift that law-trained readers actually expect. So, while it might be a distracting shift in any other discipline, it's actually the expectation or the convention in legal writing.

The other convention in the legal discipline—the one that might feel awkward to your high school English teacher—is that explanations of particular cases are written in the past tense. Now, again, this is a matter of writing conventions in different disciplines. The literary convention that your high school English teacher taught you was that when we write about literature, we do it in the present tense. (This is true even though you are writing about a book that was written in the distant past and that you read weeks ago.)

It might seem a natural transition, then, to write about the cases that you read in present tense. But while the literary convention requires you to write about what your read in present tense, the legal convention requires you to write about what you read in the past tense. Take a look at Example 5.3(b). It completes the case illustration from Example 5.3(a). You'll notice that not only are the facts described in the past tense but the court's holding and reasoning are described in the past tense as well.

Example 5.3(b)
Case illustration written in the past tense

Revision: A building is not a dwelling when it is not intermittently occupied at night. *State v. Eaton*, 602 P.2d 1159, 1160

(Or. App. 1979). The building in *Eaton* **was located** at a church camp and campers **occupied** it for just eight weeks each summer. *Id.* at 471. The rest of the year, the building **remained** empty. *Id.* The defendant **broke** into the building in November, three months after the building **had been abandoned** for the year. *Id.* The court **held** that eight weeks of occupation each year followed by forty-four weeks of vacancy, "where the burglary occurred months after the last occupant left," **was** not the kind of intermittent occupancy required to make the building a dwelling. *Id.* at 472.

Thus, while you should trust your instincts on much of what you know about writing and using different verb tenses, remember that you are writing in a specific discipline now. You need to become familiar and comfortable with the conventions of that discipline. In other words, you need to check to be sure that you write about legal rules in the present tense and case illustrations in the past tense. And you need to get comfortable with the tense shift.

2. Check Your Spelling

A polished document gains some of its sparkle from the fact that every word is spelled correctly. Many writers rely on their computer's spell check function to catch mistakes. But when the stakes are high and you are writing on behalf of a client, you simply cannot rely on your computer to catch your mistakes. You have to be responsible for carefully proofreading.

✍ Editing Strategy 5.4
Check for Tricky Homophones

One reason that you have to do a separate check and not rely on your computer's spell checker is that your computer won't find words that are spelled right but used wrong.

If you have carefully checked that you have chosen accurate language (see Editing Strategy 4.2), then you've probably already caught some of these tricky HOMOPHONES—words that sound the same but mean different things.

> **Grammar Reminder**
>
> **Homophones** are words that sound the same but mean different things.

Even if you have already checked once, you probably won't regret checking again. And remember that, when you're checking, you can't rely on the *sound* of the words, so you might have to slow down if you're proofreading by reading aloud. Chart 5.4 lists some homophones that might trip you up. Edit your writing with these tricky words in mind.

Chart 5.4
Homophones

aisle — isle	pair — pear
eye — I	peace — piece
be — bee	plain — plane
brake — break	poor — pour
buy — by	pray — prey
cell — sell	principal — principle
cent — scent	profit — prophet
cereal — serial	real — reel
coarse — course	right — write
complement — compliment	root — route
die — dye	sail — sale
fair — fare	sea — see
for — four	seam — seem
hair — hare	sight — site
heal — heel	sew — so
hear — here	sole — soul
him — hymn	some — sum
hole — whole	son — sun
hour — our	stair — stare
idle — idol	stationary — stationery
in — inn	steal — steel
knight — night	suite — sweet
knot — not	tail — tale
know — no	their — there — they're
made — maid	to — too — two
mail — male	toe — tow
meat — meet	waist — waste
morning — mourning	wait — weight
none — nun	way — weigh
oar — or	weak — week
one — won	wear — where

✎ Editing Strategy 5.5
Just Check

Checking your spelling yourself rather than relying on a spell checker can be time consuming, and it often comes at a time when you are in a rush to finish the writing that you're working on. But slow down. Just check.

If you do, you'll likely find funny typos that your autocorrect and spell check didn't find. (You meant *to the* but typed *tot he*.) Or you'll find words that your autocorrect tried to fix for you but fixed incorrectly. (You meant to describe the encounter that your client was *involved* in but wrote *evolved* instead: "These combined factors indicate that, unlike the defendant in *Royer*, Mr. Ramsey was *evolved* in a consensual encounter.")

While these kinds of typos are a little funny when you find them yourself, they are embarrassing when someone else finds them for you. And they can be costly if they make your reader doubt whether you were careful.

The Hyphen as a Matter of Spelling?

The way you use a hyphen is almost as much a matter of spelling as it is a matter of punctuation.

Because whether you hyphenate a word is often a matter of spelling, you can consult the dictionary to figure out whether a compound word needs to be hyphenated or not. And consulting a dictionary is most often a good idea. (Water-repellent is hyphenated. Waterproof is not. Who knew?)

The only other thing to keep in mind with hyphens is that you should use them when you use two or more words to work together as an adjective before a noun (*first-degree burglary*). But those very same words together after the noun don't need a hyphen (*burglary in the first degree*).

---

3. Check Your Punctuation

The final step in polishing your writing is checking to make sure that your work is perfectly punctuated. Once again, while you may be tempted to rely on your computer's grammar checker to catch punctuation mistakes, relying exclusively on the grammar checker just won't work. In fact, your computer's grammar checker is probably even more unreliable than your computer's spell checker. You need to know the rules of punctuation, and then make sure you use those rules carefully when you write. Put them to use again when you do your final polishing.

✐ Editing Strategy 5.6
Check Commas

Commas are probably the most used—and most misused—of all punctuation marks. To make sure that you are using rather than misusing commas, you should know the major comma rules inside and out. This editing strategy covers five of the major rules.

While you will inevitably run into situations that these five rules don't cover (e.g., you can actually sometimes use a comma simply to prevent confusion), having a handle on the major rules will help you maneuver most comma-related punctuation problems easily. And if you really do know these rules inside out, you'll have no problem identifying the situations that should send you looking for a more detailed description of the lesser known rules.

✍ 5.6-1. Use a comma and a coordinating conjunction to join independent clauses

You already know that an independent clause is, essentially, a full sentence. In other words, an independent clause has everything that it needs to be a sentence and either stands alone or *could* stand alone as a sentence.

Writing would get pretty dull, however, if every sentence consisted of no more than a single independent clause. So, writers sometimes link multiple independent clauses together with two simple tools—a comma and a coordinating conjunction. (Now, don't get crazy here and forget that piling too many independent clauses into a single sentence can create all kinds of problems. See Editing Strategy 3.7.)

Any time that you see two independent clauses joined with a coordinating conjunction (e.g., *and*, *or*, *but*—see Chart 3.7(1) for a complete list of coordinating conjunctions), you need to be sure that you've placed a comma before that coordinating conjunction. In Example 5.6-1(a), notice how the revision joins two separate sentences (in other words, two independent clauses) with a comma and a coordinating conjunction.

Example 5.6-1(a)
Two sentences edited by combining independent clauses with a comma and a conjunction

Draft: The St. Vincent de Paul Society placed a temporary stairway next to the trailer. *State v. Nollen*, 100 P.3d 788, 788 (Or. App. 2004). It also placed permanent signs near the trailer advertising it as a donation collection station. *Id.*

Revision: The St. Vincent de Paul Society placed a temporary stairway next to the trailer, **and** it also placed permanent signs near the trailer advertising it as a donation collection station. *State v. Nollen*, 100 P.3d 788, 788 (Or. App. 2004).

While this comma rule is straightforward, writers often run afoul of the rule by using a comma with every coordinating conjunction they see. Take a look at Example 5.6-1(b). Does the draft sentence seem remarkably similar to the revision sentence in the last example?

Example 5.6-1(b)
Sentence revised by omitting comma where the clauses are not independent

Draft: The St. Vincent de Paul Society placed a temporary stairway next to the trailer, and also placed permanent signs near the trailer advertising it as a donation collection station. *State v. Nollen*, 100 P.3d 788, 788 (Or. App. 2004).

Revision: The St. Vincent de Paul Society placed a temporary stairway next to the trailer and also placed permanent signs near the trailer advertising it as a donation collection station. *State v. Nollen*, 100 P.3d 788, 788 (Or. App. 2004).

You have to look closely to see the subtle but crucial difference. In the draft sentence in 5.6-1(b), the second part of the sentence has no subject. *It*—referring to St. Vincent de Paul Society—should be the subject, but the writer has omitted it.

Because the second part of the sentence is missing a subject, it cannot stand on its own the way that an independent clause must. If you tried to make a sentence out of it, you would create a sentence fragment. (The sentence fragment would read, "Also placed permanent signs near the trailer advertising it as a donation collection station.")

Because the coordinating conjunction in Example 5.6-1(b) isn't joining independent clauses, the revision correctly omits the comma.

The best way to approach editing for this comma rule is to look for coordinating conjunctions (remember FANBOYS). Anytime you see one, check to see whether the two parts of the sentence it joins are actually independent clauses. If they are, you need a comma. If they aren't, you don't need a comma. Just make sure none of the other comma rules apply!

✍ 5.6-2. Use a comma after an introductory clause or phrase

Commas allow writers to join together the parts of a sentence without confusing the reader. For example, commas join introductory clauses or phrases to the rest of a sentence. In that case, a comma sits just after the introduction to let the reader know that the introductory stuff is finished and now the main part of the sentence is beginning.

Take a look at Example 5.6-2(a). Notice how the comma gives the reader a little break between the introduction and the rest of the sentence. The break allows her to pause to understand what she's read so that she's better able to understand how it fits with the main clause of the sentence.

Example 5.6-2(a)
Sentence with a comma after an introductory clause

Revision: While Mr. Young did not have the opportunity to withdraw from the altercation, he likely adopted an active or aggressive role indicative of an active participant.

Introductory clauses and phrases often fall into one of two categories. First, introductory clauses and phrases often function as adverbs. Remember that an adverb's job is to modify a verb. An introductory clause or phrase that's functioning as an adverb is telling the reader *when, where, how*, or *why* the main action of the sentence occurred.

Take a look at Example 5.6-2(b). The introduction is an adverb. It's telling the reader when the main action of the sentence—Mr. Young falling backward—happened. It was *after that first and only physical contact*. The comma then lets the reader know that the main part of the sentence is about to begin and she's about to find out what the real action is.

Example 5.6-2(b)
Sentence with a comma after an introductory phrase that functions as an adverb

Revision: After that first and only physical contact, Mr. Young fell backward into a table and sustained serious injuries.

Grammar Reminder

A **participial phrase** is a phrase that that contains a verbal—a verb that does not function as the verb. In a participial phrase, the verbal is always an *-ing* or *-ed/en* word that is functioning as an adjective.

Second, introductory clauses and phrases can be PARTICIPIAL PHRASES that function as adjectives. (A participial phrase sounds scary but it's just an *-ing* word or an *-ed/-en* word that's acting like an adjective instead of doing its typical job as a verb.) Remember that an adjective's job is to modify a noun. So when a participial phrase serves as an introduction, the comma tells the reader that she's about to meet the noun that she's been hearing so much about.

Look at Example 5.6-2(c). The introduction is a participial phrase functioning as an adjective.

Example 5.6-2(c)
Sentence with a comma after an introductory phrase functioning as an adjective

Revision: Thinking Mr. Young might slap her and hurt her, Ms. Green punched Mr. Young in the jaw.

Notice how in Example 5.6-2(c), the word *thinking*, which is usually a verb, is acting like an adjective. It's describing *Ms. Green*. The comma tells the reader, at just the right moment, that she's going to meet this person who was *thinking Mr. Young might slap her and hurt her*.

Adverbs and adjectives that introduce a sentence almost always need to be followed by a comma. (If the clause or phrase is short and omitting the comma won't confuse the reader, you can get rid of it.) But there are other introductory word groups that you should look out for. When a transitional expression starts a sentence, it should be set off with a comma as well. Chart 2.4 lists common transitional words and phrases, such as *in addition, likewise*, and *on the other hand*.

One way of finding introductory clauses and phrases is to read your work aloud to yourself. While this approach isn't perfect, it will often allow you to hear places where you naturally pause. When you hear that pause, take a closer look and decide if you've got an introductory clause or phrase that needs to be followed by a comma.

✍ 5.6-3. Use a comma between all items in a series

A third major rule of commas can be summarized by simply saying that you need to use commas when you make lists. Any time you have a list of three or more things (whether those things are single words, phrases, or whole clauses) you need to separate that list with commas. Example 5.6-3(a) shows how commas separate out the three words—*owners, relatives*, and *guests*—that make up the list.

Example 5.6-3(a)
Sentence with commas between items in a series

Revision: Like the owners, relatives, and guests in *McDonald*, Ms. Carlson occupies the mobile bakery at irregular intervals.

This comma rule would be the easiest comma rule of all if not for the slippery final comma. That final comma in the series—sometimes called the serial or Oxford comma—is seen by some writers as optional. That some writers use it and some writers do not seems to depend on the discipline (journalists never use it) and stylistic preference. The problem for legal writers is that there doesn't seem to be a rule or even consensus in the legal writing discipline, and stylistic preference can be tricky when you're writing for so many varied audiences.

Even without clear rules for legal writers about that serial comma, there are two good reasons for you to always use a serial comma. First, using the serial comma is sometimes necessary to avoid confusing your reader. Take a look at Example 5.6-3(b). In the draft sentence, the writer might mean that Mr. Malmud gave his third cousin his property *and* his houses *and* his warehouses. But it is also possible that the writer means that Mr. Malmud gave his third cousin his property, which consists of his houses and his warehouses. The revision sentence clarifies the writer's meaning.

Example 5.6-3(b)
Sentence revised by including a serial comma to clarify meaning

Draft: Our client, Sam Malmud, willed to his third cousin all of his property, houses and warehouses.

Revision: Our client, Sam Malmud, willed to his third cousin all of his property, houses, and warehouses.

The second reason to always use a serial comma is that it will result in consistent comma use. Some writers leave the serial comma out as a general rule but then use it when it helps to avoid confusing their readers. But using the serial comma only when it's necessary to avoid confusion will ultimately result in some inconsistency. And your reader may wonder about that inconsistency. Was it purposeful or was it a typo?

Take another look at the draft sentence in Example 5.6-3(b). If the writer actually meant that Mr. Malmud gave his third cousin his property, which consists only of his houses and his warehouses, then that sentence is already perfectly punctuated. But if the writer has played it fast and loose with the way he uses serial commas, then the reader will be left to wonder at the writer's meaning. Play it safe and use that serial comma consistently.

The Ultimate Editing Tool

When it comes to editing, one editing tool is too important to overlook. That powerful editing tool is called "the complete rewrite." Now, the complete rewrite won't work for a whole document. Despite the temptation, throwing everything out and starting again is almost never a good idea. But the rewrite works great at the sentence level.

Here's how the complete rewrite works. If you are wrestling with a comma in a sentence and simply cannot figure out how to avoid the ambiguity that you've created, rewrite the sentence. So, "Our client, Sam Malmud, willed to his third cousin all of his property, houses and warehouses" can become "Our client, Sam Malmud, willed to his third cousin all of his property, which consisted exclusively of houses and warehouses." Your rewrite avoids the sticky comma question and, while it may be a bit wordier, it's definitely clear. Problem solved.

The complete rewrite should be used strategically and judiciously, but when used right, it can save a writer's sanity.

✍ 5.6-4. Use a comma between coordinate adjectives

You already know that commas play an important role in any list. It turns out that they play a really important role with lists of COORDINATE ADJECTIVES. Coordinate adjectives each modify the noun separately. The simple punctuation rule is that coordinate adjectives should be separated by commas.

> **Grammar Reminder**
> **Coordinate adjectives**
> are two or more adjectives that work together to describe the same noun.

Take a look at Example 5.6-4(a). The officer in that example is described as *impatient* and *angry* and *armed*. She was each of those things separately, so together they are coordinate adjectives. Those descriptive words—those adjectives—should be separated by commas as they are in the revision sentence.

Example 5.6-4(a)
Sentence revised so commas separate coordinative adjectives

Draft: The **impatient angry armed** officer approached Mr. Ramsey on the street in the middle of the night.

Revision: The **impatient, angry, armed** officer approached Mr. Ramsey on the street in the middle of the night.

To get this comma rule right, you have to be sure that you are differentiating between coordinate adjectives and CUMULATIVE ADJECTIVES. While coordinate adjectives modify the noun separately, cumulative adjectives modify the noun together.

> **Grammar Reminder**
> **Cumulative adjectives**
> are two or more adjectives that each describe the same noun.

Now take a look now at Example 5.6-4(b). In that example, the adjectives *two* and *ragged* are not coordinate—they don't work separately. Instead, they work together. Mr. Ramsey didn't hand the officer identification that was *two* and *ragged*. He handed the officer *two ragged* pieces of identification. The adjectives *two* and *ragged* are cumulative, so they are not separated by a comma.

Example 5.6-4(b)
Sentence revised so that no commas separate cumulative adjectives

Draft: Mr. Ramsey gave the police officer **two, ragged** pieces of identification.

Revision: Mr. Ramsey gave the police officer **two ragged** pieces of identification.

Because understanding this comma rule means understanding the difference between coordinate and cumulative adjectives, here's a trick for differentiating between the two: coordinate adjectives can be separated by the word *and* ("impatient and angry and armed" works) while cumulative adjectives cannot ("two and ragged" does not work). So, anytime you see multiple adjectives clumped together in a single sentence, test them to see whether they could be separated by the word *and*. If they can, they are coordinate adjectives, and you should use commas to join them.

✐ 5.6-5. Use a comma to set off nonrestrictive elements

The final entry on the list of the most important comma rules is that you must use commas to set off nonrestrictive elements in a sentence. This comma rule always sounds more daunting than it really is. This rule loses a little of its ability to intimidate with one more look at modifiers (Editing Strategies 3.8 and 4.9 through 4.11 look at modifiers in a slightly different context).

Remember that modifiers are words, phrases, or clauses that describe something. When the modifier's job is to describe a noun or a pronoun, that modifier can be either restrictive or nonrestrictive. If the modifier is essential to the sentence, we say that it is "restrictive." If the modifier isn't essential to the sentence, then we say that it is "nonrestrictive."

Describing Nouns and Pronouns:
The Hardworking Adjective's Job

Modifiers typically have just one job. They describe things. When a modifier's job is to describe a noun or a pronoun, we call the modifier an adjective.

Adjectives can come in clauses. Adjective clauses always follow the word that they modify and begin with a relative pronoun. (For more on dependent clauses and relative pronouns, look back at Editing Strategy 3.8.) For instance, in the sentence — *The contract,* **which Dr. Blackstone** *signed upon her employment, contained a covenant not to compete —* the adjective clause — *which Dr. Blackstone signed upon her employment* — is a clause modifying (or describing) the noun — *contract.*

Adjectives can also come in phrases. Prepositional phrases function as adjectives. (For more on prepositional phrases, look back at Editing Strategy 3.9.) For instance, in the sentence — *The medical practice, **with its aggressive client development strategy,** was careful to prevent former doctors from taking its clients* — the prepositional phrase — *with its aggressive client development strategy* — is functioning as an adjective modifying (or describing) the noun — *medical practice.*

Finally, appositives kind of function as adjectives. But rather than modifying the noun, an appositive renames it. For instance, in the sentence — *Dr. Blackstone, **a gifted artist,** did not want to be stifled by a covenant not to compete* — the appositive — *a gifted artist* — renames the noun — *Dr. Blackstone.* (Appositives deserve a mention here, though, because they can be either restrictive or nonrestrictive and thus have to follow the comma rules just like adjective clauses and phrases.)

Look at Example 5.6-5(a). In that example, the modifier — *that allowed her to perform the most sophisticated plastic surgeries* — is essential to the meaning of the sentence. Dr. Corliss didn't just provide Dr. Blackstone with any kind of training. She provided her a very specific kind of training — *training that allowed her to perform the most sophisticated plastic surgeries.* If the writer removed the modifier from the sentence, the whole meaning of the sentence would change. So, the modifier is essential to the sentence and thus a restrictive modifier. Because it is a restrictive modifier, it shouldn't be set apart from the rest of the sentence with a comma.

Example 5.6-5(a)
Sentence with restrictive modifier properly punctuated

Revision: Dr. Corliss hired Dr. Blackstone and provided her with training **that allowed her to perform the most sophisticated plastic surgeries.**

On the other hand, take a look at Example 5.6-5(b). In that example, the modifier — *who had just graduated from medical school when Arizona Rim hired her* — is not essential to the sentence. If the writer removed the modifier from the sentence, some detail might be lost but the sentence would remain essentially the same. So the modifier is nonrestrictive. Because it is nonrestrictive, it can — and should — be set apart from the rest of the sentence with a comma.

> **Example 5.6-5(b)**
> **Sentence with nonrestrictive modifier properly punctuated**
>
> Revision: At the start of her employment with Arizona Rim, Dr. Blackstone, **who had just graduated from medical school when Arizona Rim hired her,** signed an employment agreement that included a covenant not to compete.

Often, distinguishing a nonrestrictive modifier from a restrictive modifier can be simple. You can just ask whether the modifier is essential to the meaning of the sentence. If it is, then the modifier is restrictive. If the modifier isn't essential to the meaning of the sentence, then it is nonrestrictive.

But sometimes, distinguishing between a restrictive and a nonrestrictive modifier requires you to think more carefully about what you actually mean. Consider the difference between the sentences in Example 5.6-5(c) and 5.6-5(d). Both of the sentences are grammatically correct. They just mean different things.

In Example 5.6-5(c), the phrase *who was still allowed to sell mattresses* is restrictive. It tells the reader that there were multiple sales associates described in the *Bed Mart* case. (One was Bob, and he was allowed to sell mattresses. The other was Tom, and he was not allowed to sell mattresses.) Dr. Blackstone is like the one who was still allowed to sell mattresses (Bob) rather than the one who was no longer allowed to sell mattresses (Tom).

> **Example 5.6-5(c)**
> **Sentence with restrictive modifier properly punctuated**
>
> Revision: Like the mattress sales associate in *Bed Mart* **who was still allowed to sell mattresses,** Dr. Blackstone can still continue to work in her chosen profession.

By contrast, in Example 5.6-5(d), the phrase *who was still allowed to sell mattresses* is nonrestrictive. It tells the reader that there was just one sales associate in *Bed Mart* (just Bob) and then simply adds some information about that particular sales associate.

> **Example 5.6-5(d)**
> **Sentence with restrictive modifier**
>
> Revision: Like the mattress sales associate in *Bed Mart*, **who was still allowed to sell mattresses,** Dr. Blackstone can still continue to work in her chosen profession.

The best way to approach editing for this comma rule is to look for modifiers, particularly adjective clauses, phrases functioning as adjective, and appositives (see Describing Nouns and Pronouns: The Hardworking Adjective's Job). When you find one of these modifiers, decide whether it's essential to the sentence. If it isn't essential, set it off with commas.

✍ Editing Strategy 5.7
Check Semicolons

Maybe one reason that commas are misused is that writers often enlist a comma to do the job of a semicolon. The semicolon is really the right punctuation mark for the job when the writer is (1) joining closely related independent clauses without a conjunction or (2) connecting complex items in a series. These jobs sound a lot like those in which commas case be used (see Editing Strategy 5.6-1 and 5.6-3), but read on for more on why the semicolon sometimes is the punctuation mark for the job. And note the limitations on the situations: the clauses have to be *closely related* and the items in the series have to be *complex*.

✍ 5.7-1. Use a semicolon to join independent clauses

A comma and a coordinating conjunction can join two independent clauses (see Editing Strategy 5.6-1), but if the two independent clauses are closely enough related, you can actually replace the comma and the coordinating conjunction with a semicolon. Take a look at Example 5.7-1(a). Notice how in the revised sentence, the semicolon takes the place of the comma and the coordinating conjunction *and*.

> **In Defense of the Comma**
>
> To be fair to the comma, it can, most of the time, do the job of a semi-colon as long as the writer uses it right.
>
> For example, the comma can join two independent clauses as long as it has a coordinating conjunction to assist.
>
> The problem is that some writers try to join independent clauses with *just* a comma. This doesn't work and creates that dreaded comma splice that your English teachers warned you about.

Example 5.7-1(a)
Sentence where semicolon replaces comma and coordinating conjunction

Draft: The St. Vincent de Paul Society placed a temporary stairway next to the trailer, **and** it also placed permanent signs near the trailer advertising it as a donation collection station. *State v. Nollen*, 196 Or. App. 141, 143 (2004).

Revision: The St. Vincent de Paul Society placed a temporary stairway next to the trailer; it also placed permanent signs near the trailer advertising it as a donation collection station. *State v. Nollen*, 196 Or. App. 141, 143 (2004).

But before you start replacing every comma and coordinating conjunction with a semicolon, you should think a bit about the semicolon's limitations.

First, a semicolon can join only independent clauses that are clearly closely related. In other words, your reader should be able to see immediately the relationship between the two clauses without the help of a coordinating conjunction or any other transition. Take a look at Example 5.7-1(b). Notice how the draft sentence lacks the clear connection necessary for the reader to understand the point the writer is trying to make. A semicolon won't work. The revision splits the independent clauses into separate sentences and adds a word of transition to make the writer's meaning clear.

Example 5.7-1(b)
Sentence where independent clauses are not closely enough related to be joined with a semicolon, revised by replacing the semicolon with a period

Draft: As in *Bed Mart*, where the employer could prove that it took six months to replace a mattress sales associate, Arizona Rim can prove that it will take nine months to replace Dr. Blackstone; the covenant not to compete restricts Dr. Blackstone for practicing for fourteen months.

Revision: As in *Bed Mart*, where the employer could prove that it took six months to replace a mattress sales associate, Arizona Rim can prove that it will take nine months to replace Dr. Blackstone. However, the covenant not to compete restricts Dr. Blackstone for practicing for fourteen months.

Sometimes, though, two independent clauses are just begging to be joined with a semicolon. In Example 5.7-1(c), either of the draft sentences will work. They are both well written and properly punctuated. But the revision sentence has the greatest impact.

Example 5.7-1(c)
Sentences with independent clauses punctuated three different ways

Correct Draft: Arizona Rim will be able to replace Dr. Blackstone in just nine months. It is attempting to restrict competition by preventing her from practicing for fourteen months.

Better Draft:	Arizona Rim will be able to replace Dr. Blackstone in just nine months, but it is attempting to restrict competition by preventing her from practicing for fourteen months.
Revision:	Arizona Rim will be able to replace Dr. Blackstone in just nine months; it is attempting to restrict competition by preventing her from practicing for fourteen months.

This brings us to the semicolon's second limitation; the semicolon is a bit dramatic as punctuation marks go. It draws attention to the relationship between the two independent clauses in a way that a comma and a coordinating conjunction simply do not. (Did you notice that the revision sentence in Example 5.7-1(c) is the most dramatic of the three options?) Use the semicolon a bit sparingly so that it retains its drama.

The semicolon has a few other limitations. But these limitations essentially just require you to use the semicolon correctly. Don't try to join a dependent clause with the rest of the sentence using a semicolon. (The semicolon can join only *independent* clauses, not dependent ones.) And don't use a semicolon between independent clauses joined by a coordinating conjunction. (Remember, the semicolon has to replace the comma *and* the coordinating conjunction.)

✍ 5.7-2. Use a semicolon between items in a series containing internal punctuation

Another place where the semicolon sometimes has to do some heavy lifting is in a list. You already know that you need commas when you make lists (see Editing Strategy 5.6-3), but sometimes a comma is not enough. More specifically, when your list is long and complicated enough that it has internal punctuation, then you need to use semicolons rather than commas between the items in the list.

Example 5.7-2(a) demonstrates this problem. Notice that in the draft sentence the items in the list are all punctuated with commas. To try to *also* separate the items in the list with commas is just too much and too confusing. The revision sentence fixes this confusion by separating the items in the list with semicolons.

> **Example 5.7-2(a)**
> **Sentence with a list with internal punctuation, revised so the list is separated by semicolons**
>
> Draft: Arizona Rim has offices in Flagstaff, Arizona, Albuquerque, New Mexico, and Pasadena, California.
>
> Revision: Arizona Rim has offices in Flagstaff, Arizona; Albuquerque, New Mexico; and Pasadena, California.

Because most writers use semicolons rarely, if at all, you may actually discover that editing for semicolons is a matter of finding places to use them rather than making sure you've used them correctly. So, as you're editing, rather than looking for semicolons, look for (1) sentences that may benefit from being linked by a semicolon rather than a comma and conjunction and (2) lists that may need to be punctuated with semicolons rather than commas. When you find a place where you really need a semicolon rather than a comma, use the semicolon.

✍ Editing Strategy 5.8
Check Colons

Colons are quite useful in numbers. You use them to show proportion — *5:1* — and to indicate hours and minutes — *3:37 p.m.* They are primarily used in writing as a signal to readers to pay attention to what comes next.

Colons typically tell readers to pay attention to two things: lists and quotations. The important thing to remember is that the colon must follow an independent clause (remember, an independent clause could stand on its own as a sentence). If the clause before the colon isn't an independent clause, then the colon is sitting somewhere it doesn't belong.

Take a look at Example 5.8(a). In the draft, the part of the sentence that comes before the colon is not an independent clause. In the revision, the writer has added two words — *three things* — to the opening clause to make it independent, and just like that, the sentence becomes grammatically correct.

> **Example 5.8(a)**
> **Sentence with colon edited so that colon follows an independent clause**
>
> Draft: To determine whether a covenant not to compete is reasonable, courts consider: the covenant's restraint on

> the scope of employment, the duration of the covenant, and the geographic area covered by the covenant. *Valley Medical Specialists v. Farber*, 982 P.2d 1277, 1281 (Ariz. 1999).
>
> Revision: To determine whether a covenant not to compete is reasonable, courts consider three things: the covenant's restraint on the scope of employment, the duration of the covenant, and the geographic area covered by the covenant. *Valley Medical Specialists v. Farber*, 982 P.2d 1277, 1281 (Ariz. 1999).

The same rules hold true for colons used to set off quotations. If the writer has used an independent clause to introduce the quotation, then using a colon is appropriate. If, however, the writer has incorporated the quote into her sentence, then she can't use a colon. (For more on the different ways to introduce and punctuate a quotation, see Editing Strategy 5.9.)

In the draft sentence in Example 5.8(b), the writer hasn't introduced the quotation with an independent clause, so the use of the colon in inappropriate. With a few minor changes to the draft sentence, the writer has introduced the quotation with an independent clause. Look closely. Do you see how the first part of the revised sentence could actually stand alone as a sentence with nothing more? Thus, the colon becomes the right punctuation mark.

Example 5.8(b)
Sentence with colon edited so that the colon follows an independent clause

Draft: The language in Dr. Blackstone's covenant not to compete states that: "[f]or fourteen months after the cessation of employment with Arizona Rim for any reason, Dr. Blackstone agrees not to perform cosmetic surgeries within the city of Flagstaff, AZ, or within forty miles of the city of Flagstaff, AZ."

Revision: The language in Dr. Blackstone's covenant not to compete restricts her ability to pursue her profession: "For fourteen months after the cessation of employment with Arizona Rim for any reason, Dr. Blackstone agrees not to perform cosmetic surgeries within the city of Flagstaff, AZ, or within forty miles of the city of Flagstaff, AZ."

Like semicolons, colons are used infrequently. Before using one, look to the left of the colon to be sure that you see a complete sentence. With that one simple check, you'll be sure that you're telling your reader to pay attention to what follows the colon rather than paying attention to the way you've mistreated the colon.

Editing Strategy 5.9
Check Quotation Marks

Quotations are an important part of legal writing. Undoubtedly, the citation manual that you're working with goes into quite a bit of detail about how and when to use quotations and how to cite them properly. But your citation manual may not go into detail about punctuating quotations. If your citation manual doesn't give you detail about how to properly punctuate quotations, use the following guidelines as you edit your citations:

(1) **Periods and commas belong inside quotation marks.** While other disciplines and other countries may take a different approach, legal writers in the United States put periods and commas inside the quotation marks, as in Example 5.9(a).

Example 5.9(a)
Periods and commas inside the quotation marks

Revision: In *Hernandez*, the court specifically said that it would not "elevate form over substance," explaining that if the delay in filing is not prejudicial to the plaintiff, an untimely filing may be permitted. *Hernandez*, 688 F. Supp. at 562.

---

(2) **Colons and semicolons belong outside quotation marks.** This standard is fairly universal among different disciplines. Colons and semicolons belong outside the quotation marks, as in Example 5.9(b).

Example 5.9(b)
Semicolons outside the quotation marks

Revision: Mr. Reed said, "I couldn't actually see whether my wife was in the Ferris wheel car that fell"; he was, however, certain that she was a passenger on the Ferris wheel at the time of the accident.

---

(3) Question marks and exclamation points belong inside quotation marks, unless they apply to the whole sentence. Typically, question marks and exclamation marks belong inside the quotation marks, as in Example 5.9(c).

Example 5.9(c)
Exclamation point inside quotation marks

Revision: He heard someone yell, "Watch out!" before seeing the entire car fall to the ground.

However, when the question mark or exclamation point is punctuating the entire sentence, it belongs outside the quotation marks, as in Example 5.9(d).

Example 5.9(d)
Question mark outside quotation marks

Revision: Were you at the deposition when Mr. Reed said, "I couldn't actually see whether my wife was in the Ferris wheel car that fell"?

In addition to editing the quotation itself for proper punctuation, you'll also want to edit to be sure that you've properly introduced any quotations. Part of that proper introduction requires properly punctuating your introduction. To punctuate your introduction, you'll have to choose between a colon, a comma, or no punctuation at all.

Choose a colon where you've introduced the quotation with a full independent clause, as in Example 5.9(e).

Example 5.9(e)
Independent clause and colon introducing quotation

Revision: The federal removal statute lays out the timeline for filing a notice of removal: "The notice of removal of a civil action or proceeding shall be filed within thirty days after the receipt by the defendant, through service or otherwise, of a copy of the initial pleading setting forth the claim for relief upon which such action or proceeding is based...." 28 U.S.C. § 1446(b) (2006).

Choose a comma or no punctuation at all where you've incorporated the quotation into the sentence. As for choosing between a comma and no punctuation, you simply have to decide how the quotation fits into the rest of the sentence. In other words, just decide whether you would use a comma if the sentence *didn't* contain a quotation.

In Example, 5.9(f), the quotation is incorporated into the sentence and no introductory punctuation is needed, while in Example 5.9(g), the sentence requires a comma.

Example 5.9(f)
Quotation introduction with no punctuation

Revision: In *Hernandez*, the court specifically said that it would not "elevate form over substance," explaining that if the delay in filing is not prejudicial to the plaintiff, an untimely filing may be permitted. *Hernandez*, 688 F. Supp. at 562.

Example 5.9(g)
Quotation introduction punctuated with a comma

Revision: Mr. Reed was, as he put it, "terrified that my wife might be in the red car and falling to terrible injury."

✍ Editing Strategy 5.10
Check Apostrophes

Like the comma, apostrophes are also often misused. Perhaps it's their small size that makes them so easy to overlook. It might also have something to do with the different ways that they get used. Apostrophes are used in two main, completely unrelated ways: (1) in contractions to signal omissions (*it's, they're, can't*) and (2) with nouns to signal ownership or possession (*Jillian's book, the car's hood*).

Finding and fixing apostrophes that are misused in contractions is a fairly straightforward task. For most native English speakers, most contractions are a breeze (*can't, won't, shouldn't*). The contractions that tend to cause trouble are those that have homophones that *are not* contractions. For example, you can write *its* when you mean *it's* or *their* when you mean *they're*. To find and fix these, be diligent. But, if you've checked to make sure that your language is accurate (Editing Strategy 4.2) and then checked for tricky homophones (Editing Strategy 5.4) and done one more sweep for apostrophes, well, it's hard to imagine that you could be more diligent than that.

Finding and fixing apostrophe problems related to ownership and possession, however, can be a bit more difficult. To find these problems, you have to be more than diligent. You have to know some key rules about turning nouns into possessive nouns.

Five rules on apostrophes are explained below. The first is the basic rule on making nouns possessive. The next two rules will show you where to put an apostrophe in a word that ends in -s. The final two rules will show you where to put an apostrophe when there is more than one owner (or, perhaps, more appropriately, *possessor*).

(1) **Add an -'s to *any noun* that does not already end in -s.** In example 5.10(a), the noun *employer*, ends with an -*r* so, to make it possessive, the writer has an added -'s.

Example 5.10(a)
Punctuation for singular, possessive noun

Revision: Under Arizona common law, courts consider a covenant not to compete unenforceable when the restraint is greater than necessary to protect the **employer's** legitimate business interest or if the hardship to the employee and public policy outweigh that interest. *Valley Medical Specialists v. Farber*, 982 P.2d 1277, 1283 (Ariz. 1999).

Notice how in Example 5.10(a) the possessive noun *employer's* has possession or ownership of *legitimate business interest*. In some ways, the idea that the employer can possess something this abstract is strange. But, often, possession is a bit abstract. That just means that you have to be even more careful when looking for nouns that need to be possessive.

(2) **Add an -'s to *singular nouns* that end in -s or an s sound.** Even if the noun that you're trying to make possessive already ends in an -*s* (or an -*s* sound: think *Max's* trial brief), you still add an -'s *as long as the noun is singular*. In Example 5.10(b), Dr. Corliss is the noun that the writer needs to make possessive. Because there is just one Dr. Corliss (Dr. Corliss is a singular noun), the writer adds -'s, even though Dr. Corliss already ends with an -*s*.

Example 5.10(b)
Punctuation for singular, possessive noun ending in -s

Revision: Arizona Rim has suffered since the departure of Dr. Blackstone. Specifically, **Dr. Corliss's** practice has lost several patients to Dr. Blackstone.

---

(3) **Add just an apostrophe to *plural nouns* that end in -s.** When a noun is plural and already ends in -s, you just need to add the apostro-

---

What's Mines Is Mines

In English, we make nouns possessive (most of the time) by adding -'s. So, the car that belongs to Charlotte is *Charlotte's car*.

But while this -'s trick works for nouns, it is not necessary for pronouns. In English, we have a whole set of pronouns — appropriately named **possessive pronouns** — whose job it is to show ownership.

We talk about *his car* and *her car* and *that car is mine* without an apostrophe in sight.

While you probably rarely give a second thought to this complexity, it wasn't always second nature for you. If you need proof, just pay close attention the next time you hear an indignant three year old demand the return of her toy car: "It's mine's!"

phe. Take a look at Example 5.10(c). To make the plural noun *patients* possessive, the writer just needed to add an apostrophe.

Example 5.10(c)
Punctuation for plural, possessive noun ending in -*s*

Revision:　Courts generally disfavor covenants not to compete, especially among physicians, because these covenants often limit **patients'** freedom to choose their doctors and receive quality medical care. *Valley Medical Specialists*, 982 P.2d at 1281.

As if making a single noun possessive weren't complicated enough, sometimes you have to deal with people owning things together or owning the same thing, but separately. This kind of possession requires you to figure out just two more rules.

(4) Add an -'*s* to just the last noun to show joint possession. In Example 5.10(d), the writer is describing a time when Dr. Corliss and Dr. Blackstone shared a practice. It was just one practice, and they had joint possession of it. Because they had joint possession, just a single -'*s* is needed.

Example 5.10(d)
Joint possession indicated with a single apostrophe

Revision:　**Dr. Corliss and Dr. Blackstone's** practice was successful in large part because of the way in which Dr. Corliss trained Dr. Blackstone.

---

(5) Add an -'*s* to every noun to show individual possession. In Example 5.10(e), the writer is describing the current tension between Dr. Corliss and Dr. Blackstone. They now each have their own practices. No longer do they have joint possession of a single thing. They have individual possession; it just happens to be of the same kind of thing—medical practices.

Example 5.10(e)
Individual possession indicated with multiple apostrophes

Revision:　**Dr. Corliss's and Dr. Blackstone's** practices are in direct competition for patients.

If you spend a little time with these apostrophe rules, even if you don't master them, you'll know enough to know when you should go running for a resource on apostrophes.

4. Polishing and Perfection

Each step in the editing process is important. And it's important at every step along the way that you try very hard to be sure that your writing is perfect.

But the reality is that your writing won't be perfect. Writers are humans after all. And we all make mistakes.

There are a few keys to making the most of your mistakes. First, be very careful that your mistakes are really just occasional mistakes and not a pattern of carelessness. You definitely want your reader to say, "that's strange" rather than "that's typical."

Second, learn from your mistakes. When you make a mistake—and you will—add that mistake to your personal editing checklist. You'll do better next time.

Finally, forgive yourself. You will make mistakes. You'll become a better writer if you learn from those mistakes, but you'll gain nothing by dwelling on them.

Polished Writing:
The Exercises

The following text appears in a memo about burglary. Use Editing Strategies 5.1 through 5.10 to edit this passage for grammar, spelling, and punctuation.

The mobile bakery that Justin Dennison broke into is a building under Oregon law. The State can establish that a structure is a building in one of two ways: (1) by proving that the structure is a "building" in the "ordinary meaning" of that term or (2) by proving that it is a "booth, vehicle, boat, aircraft, or other structure adapted for overnight accommodation of persons or for carrying on business therein". Or. Rev. Stat. § 164.205(1) (2013). Because the van is not a building within the ordinary meaning of that term, the question is whether it is a vehicle adapted for overnight accommodation of persons or for carrying on business therein.

While the van is occasionaly used as a place of overnight accommodation, it has not been sufficiently adapted for overnight accommodation under the statue. However, it has been adapted for carrying on business. A vehicle was adapted if it was changed or modified so that it was suitable for a new or different use. *State v. Nollen*, 100 P.3d 788, 789 (Or. App. 2004). This new or different use must be a business use, which is simply: " 'a commercial or industrial enterprise.' " *Id.* (*quoting* Webster's Third New Int'l Dictionary 23 (unabridged ed. 1993)).

In *Nollen*, the court held that a semi-truck trailer was a building because it had been adapted for use as a business. *Id.* St. Vincent de Paul, a charitable organization, used the semi-truck trailer as a donation center. *Id.* at 788. A truck would tow a trailer to the transfer station, but then the driver would detach the trailer, and leave it for a period of time. *Id.* In addition to the driver leaving the trailer for a period of time St. Vincent placed a temporary stairway next to the tralier so that members of the public could walk up the stairs and into the trailer to make their donations.

Id. St. Vincent also placed large permanent signs near the trailer advertising it as a donation collection station. *Id.* According to the court, by making these changes, St. Vincent had adapted the trailer from it's ordinary use as a vehicle to use in the business of collecting and redistributing donations. *Id.* at 789. The court reasoned that, because the statute does not require that the adaptation of a vehicle be permanent, the changes to the trailer were sufficient even though the trailer was not permanently located at the transfer station. *Id.* Thus, the trailer was a building. *Id.*

On the other hand, in *State v. Scott*, 590 P.2d 743, 744 (Or. App. 1979), the court held that a railroad boxcar was not a building because it had not been modified to be used as anything other than a vehicle. In *Scott*, the defendant entered a railroad boxcar with the intent to commit a crime. *See id.* However, because the railroad boxcar was not a building, the court overturned the defendants burglary conviction. *Id.* The court noted that a boxcar could conceivably be adapted for business. *Id.* However, because the boxcar in that case had not been changed in any way from its ordinary purpose — that is, because it was still simply a "structure on wheels designed for the storage of goods and their transportation" — the court held that it was not a building. *Id.*

Here, the mobile bakery that Mr. Dennison entered is a building because it has been adapted for carrying on business. The mobile bakery which was originally simply a utility van has been changed and modified, much in the same way that the trailer in *Nollen* was modified and stands in contrast to the boxcar in *Scott*. Like the trailer in *Nollen*, which was detached from the truck, that towed it, the van's awning was open and extending from the side of the van and chairs were positioned under that awning. These changes make both the trailer in *Nollen* and the mobile bakery unsuitable four use as a vehicle while they are in business; but Ms. Carlson has made even more changes to the van, which make it markedly different from the boxcar in *Scott*. Unlike in *Scott*, where there was no evidence that the boxcar had been modified at all, there is ample evidence of modifications to the van. Ms. Carlson modified the van by putting down laminate flooring, adding refrigerator space for her products, and she added a sink, and small bathroom. All of these changes demonstrate that the van has been adapted for a new purpose.

Moreover, the changes to the mobile bakery make it suitable for use in a commercial or industrial enterprise. In other words, the van, like the truck in *Nollen* but unlike the boxcar in *Scott*, is suitable for use as a business. Just like St. Vincent, which placed stares next to the donation truck so that patrons could enter the trailer and leave their donations, Ms. Carlson opens the van doors and the side window to create a service counter, and she opens the awning at the side of the van so that patrons can relax in chairs in its shade. In addition, like St. Vincent advertising the trailer as the location of its business, Ms. Carlson advertises the mobile bakery as the location of her business. St. Vincent de Paul placed permanent signs near the trailer advertising it as a donation center. While Ms. Carlson has no permanent signs to advertise her van as a mobile bakery she does display signs listing the cupcake flavors and prices, and she plays music from a portable speaker. Both the temporary cupcake signs and the music serve a similar purpose to the St. Vincent's permanent signs—advertising a business. In fact, the changes that Ms. Carlson made to the van are presumably the kinds of changes that the court in *Scott* alluded to when it suggested that a vehicle could conceivably be modified so that it could be used for business purposes. Ms. Carlsons' van is now much more than just a "structure on wheels designed for the storage of goods and their transportation." Through the changes, it has become suitable for use as a business and thus is a building. Unlike the lack of changes to the railroad boxcar in *Scott* and like the changes to the trailer in *Nollen*, the changes to the mobile bakery adapted the vehicle from its ordinary use for transportation to use in Ms. Carlson's bakery business.

However, Mr. Denison may argue that the changes Ms. Carlson made to the mobile cupcake van were not as significant as the changes made to the trailer in *Nollen*. He may argue that, unlike the detached trailer in *Nollen*, which was detached from the truck, the van really continued to be a vehicle. However, because their is no statutory requirement that the adaptation of the vehicle be permanent, this argument is unlikely to succeed. So even though the van might have occasionally been simply transportation like the railroad car in *Scott*, while it was parked and doing business as a mobile bakery, it was a building.

Appendix A

Editing Checklist

Coherent Writing

- ❑ 2.1 Check the beginning of each section of your document for an introduction
- ❑ 2.2 Check the beginning of each new legal analysis or argument for an introduction
- ❑ 2.3 Check the beginning of each paragraph for a topic sentence
- ❑ 2.4 Check for transitional words and phrases
- ❑ 2.5 Check for substantive transitions

Vigorous Writing

- ❑ 3.1 Check for abstract nouns at the beginning of a sentence
- ❑ 3.2 Check for *it is* and *there are* at the beginning of a sentence
- ❑ 3.3 Check for vague verbs
- ❑ 3.4 Check for passive voice
- ❑ 3.5 Check for nominalizations
- ❑ 3.6 Check for long sentences
- ❑ 3.7 Check for too many independent clauses in a single sentence
- ❑ 3.8 Check for too many dependent clauses in a single sentence
- ❑ 3.9 Check for too many prepositional phrases in a sentence
- ❑ 3.10 Check for wordy phrases

Clear Writing

- ☐ 4.1   Check that language is clear
- ☐ 4.2   Check that language is accurate
- ☐ 4.3   Check that language is consistent
- ☐ 4.4   Check for ambiguous pronouns
- ☐ 4.5   Check for remote pronouns
- ☐ 4.6   Check that pronouns and their antecedents agree
- ☐ 4.7   Check that subjects and verbs agree
- ☐ 4.8   Check that subjects and verbs are close together
- ☐ 4.9   Check for misplaced modifiers
- ☐ 4.10 Check for dangling modifiers
- ☐ 4.11 Check for squinting modifiers

Polished Writing

- ☐ 5.1   Check for sentence fragments
- ☐ 5.2   Check for parallel structure
- ☐ 5.3   Check verb tense
- ☐ 5.4   Check for tricky homophones
- ☐ 5.5   Just check (your spelling)
- ☐ 5.6   Check commas
  - ☐ 5.6-1   Use a comma and a coordinating conjunction to join independent clauses.
  - ☐ 5.6-2   Use a comma after an introductory clause or phrase.
  - ☐ 5.6-3   Use a comma between all items in a series.
  - ☐ 5.6-4   Use a comma between coordinate adjectives.
  - ☐ 5.6-5   Use a comma to set off nonrestrictive elements.
- ☐ 5.7   Check semicolons
  - ☐ 5.7-1   Use a semicolon to join independent clauses.
  - ☐ 5.7-2   Use a semicolon between items in a series containing internal punctuation.
- ☐ 5.8   Check colons
- ☐ 5.9   Check quotation marks
- ☐ 5.10 Check apostrophes

Appendix B

Grammar Reminders

Adjective: An adjective is a word that modifies or describes a noun or a pronoun. You can spot adjectives because they usually answer questions like *which one? What kind of? How many?*

>   **Coordinate adjectives:** Coordinate adjectives are just two or more adjectives that each describe the same noun.

>   **Cumulative adjectives:** Cumulative adjectives are two or more adjectives that work together to describe the same noun.

Antecedent: An antecedent is the noun that a pronoun refers back to.

Clause: Clauses, unlike phrases, look just like sentences. They have subjects and verbs. They can be independent or dependent.

>   **Independent Clause:** An independent clause is a full sentence pattern—in other words, it has everything it needs to be a sentence—and it either stands alone as a sentence or *could* stand alone as a sentence.

>   **Dependent Clause:** A dependent clause, like an independent clause, has everything that it needs to be a sentence (a subject and a verb). But a dependent clause, unlike an independent clause, is linked to the rest of the sentence in a way that makes it *depend* on the rest of the sentence for its meaning. In other words, it can't stand alone.

Conjunction: A conjunction is a word used to join words, phrases, or clauses. Different kinds of conjunctions express different relationships between the words, phrases, or clauses that they join.

>   **Coordinating Conjunction:** Coordinating conjunctions hook together two equal grammatical elements—two words, two phrases, or two clauses.

>   **Subordinating Conjunction:** Subordinating conjunctions introduce a clause but demonstrate how it is lesser than—subordinate to—the rest of the sentence.

Homophones: Homophones are words that sound the same but mean different things.

Modifier: Modifier is the generic term for any word, phrase, or clause that modifies or qualifies something. Modifiers are usually either adjectives used to modify or describe a noun or pronoun or adverbs that are used to modify or qualify a verb, an adjective, or another adverb.

> **Restrictive Modifier:** A restrictive modifier is a modifier that further defines the word that it is modifying and therefore contains information that is essential to the sentence.

> **Nonrestrictive Modifier:** A nonrestrictive modifier is a modifier that simply gives additional information about a word that has already been clearly defined. It's helpful, but not necessary, in the sentence.

Noun: A noun is a word that names a person, place, or thing. A concrete noun is, most often, a person, place, or physical object (think: judge, defendant, court, written judicial opinion). An abstract noun, on the other hand, is most often an idea or concept (think: liability, negligence, reasonableness).

> **Count Nouns:** Count nouns refer to persons, places, and things that can be counted, like bottles.

> **Noncount Nouns/Mass Nouns:** Noncount nouns refer to things or abstractions that can't be counted, like champagne.

> **Collective Noun:** A collective noun is a noun that names a class or group, like company.

Nominalization: A nominalization is a verb that is functioning as a noun.

Passive Voice/Truncated Passive Voice: The passive voice is a verb form that inverts a sentence so that the actor receives the action. It is formed by combining a form of the *to be* verb with a past participle. Sentences written in the passive voice hide the logical subject of the sentence in a prepositional phrase. Sentences written in the truncated passive voice omit the prepositional phrase with the logical subject altogether.

Preposition: A preposition is a word (see Chart 3.9(1)) that is grouped with a noun to form a prepositional phrase.

Phrase: A phrase, unlike a clause, doesn't look like a sentence. Phrases are just groups of at least two words that are linked together but don't have a subject and a verb. Phrases come in lots of different forms.

> **Participial Phrase:** A participial phrase is a phrase that that contains a verbal—a verb that does not function as the verb. In a participial phrase, the verbal is always an *–ing* or *–ed/en* word that is functioning as an adjective.

> **Prepositional Phrase:** A prepositional phrase is a phrase that is made up of a preposition (e.g., *at, by, for, of*) and a noun that gram-

marians call the object of the preposition. Together, the preposition and the noun create a prepositional phrase and function as an adjective or an adverb.

Pronoun: A pronoun is a word that you can use in place of a noun. For example, the personal pronoun *she* can replace the noun *woman*. There are several different kinds of pronouns.

> **Indefinite Pronouns:** An indefinite pronoun is a pronoun that refers to a nonspecific person or thing (everyone, each).

> **Possessive Pronouns:** A possessive pronoun is a pronoun that indicates ownership (mine, hers).

> **Relative Pronouns:** A relative pronoun is a pronoun that introduces a dependent clause. Like all pronouns, relative pronouns allow you to link together two thoughts without repeating the noun.

Subject: The subject of a sentence names who or what the sentence is about. The subject of a sentence is, often, everything that comes before the verb. So, if you're having trouble finding the subject, switch tactics and look for the verb.

> **Compound Subject:** A compound subject is a subject that is made up of two or more simple subjects joined with a coordinating conjunction.

Verb: A verb is a word that expresses action or being. Verbs come in different forms, including past participles and present participles. The verb forms are as follows:

> **Base verb:** I *walk*.

> **-s form:** She *walks*.

> **Past tense:** I *walked*.

> **Past participle:** I *have walked*.

> **Present participle:** I *am walking*.

Appendix C

More Resources

Stephen V. Armstrong & Timothy P. Terrell, *Thinking Like a Writer: A Lawyer's Guide to Effective Writing and Editing* (3d ed. 2009).

Veda R. Charrow, Myra K. Erhard & Robert P. Charrow, *Clear and Effective Legal Writing* (4th ed. 2007).

Anne Enquist & Laurel Currie Oates, *Just Writing: Grammar, Punctuation, and Style for the Legal Writer* (4th ed. 2013).

Mignon Fogarty, *The Ultimate Writing Guide for Students* (2011).

Bryan A. Garner, *The Redbook: A Manual on Legal Style* (2d ed. 2006).

Diana Hacker, *The Bedford Handbook* (7th ed. 2009).

Joan Ames Magat, *The Lawyer's Editing Manual* (2009).

Bonnie Trenga, *The Curious Case of the Misplaced Modifier: How to Solve the Mysteries of Weak Writing* (2006).

Index

Bolded numbers indicate the page on which a grammar reminder for the term appears.